# VICTORIAN GHOST STORIES

Jo-Anne Christensen

GHOST
HOUSE

Ghost House Books

**The Publisher: Ghost House Books**
Distributed by Lone Pine Publishing

10145 – 81 Avenue                    1808 – B Street NW, Suite 140
Edmonton, AB T6E 1W9                 Auburn, WA 98001
Canada                               USA

**Website:** http://www.ghostbooks.net

**National Library of Canada Cataloguing in Publication**

Christensen, Jo-Anne
    Victorian ghost stories / Jo-Anne Christensen.

    ISBN 1-894877-35-7

    1. Ghosts. I. Title.
BF1461.C53 2004      133.1      C2004-900150-7

*Editorial Director:* Nancy Foulds
*Editorial:* Christopher Wangler, Lee Craig
*Illustrations Coordinator:* Carol Woo
*Production Coordinator:* Gene Longson
*Cover Design:* Gerry Dotto
*Layout & Production:* Chia-Jung Chang

*Photo Credits:* Every effort has been made to accurately credit sources. Any errors or omissions should be directed to the publisher for changes in future editions. The images in this book are reproduced with the kind permission of the following sources: Fortean Picture Library (p. 10: C451/28/DS2 [Derek Stafford]; p. 14: C295/69; p. 30: C599/4/DW; p. 53: C460/14/D52 [Derek Stafford]; p. 65: P034/21; p. 70: C162/1T; p. 78, 58: P004/2 [Edward Wyllie]; p. 82: C610/15/DW; p. 87: C159/2; p. 90: P093/9; p. 93: P146/33A [Gordon Wain]; p. 94: C443/24; p. 97: P014/2; Library of Congress (p. 103: USZ62-108225; p. 117: LC-DIG-cwpbh-034440; p. 123, 100: LC-USZ62-117829, (p. 131: C499/7A/AT [Andreas Trottmann]; p. 4–5, 127, 137: C499/8A/AT [Andreas Trottmann]); p. 177: HABS,CAL,38-SANFRA, 85-1).

We acknowledge the financial support of the Government of Canada through the Book Publishing Industry Development Program (BPIDP) for our publishing activities.

PC: P5

*For W. Ritchie Benedict,*
*a talented researcher and writer and a terrific*
*authority on all things that go bump in the night...*

# Contents

Acknowledgments  6

Introduction  7

## Chapter 1: Famous Phantoms

Raynham Hall's Sinister Lady  12

Willington Mill  16

A Riveting Maritime Tale  19

The Greenbrier Ghost  22

An Adventure at Versailles  26

Number 50, Berkeley Square  33

A Horror in Amherst  37

Ballechin House  47

"The Morton Case"  51

## Chapter 2: The Spiritualists

Emanuel Swedenborg  60

Andrew Jackson Davis  64

The Fox Sisters  68

Séances in High Places  73

Worth a Thousand Words: The Era of Spirit Photography  76

Lily Dale and Cassadaga: Communities of Spirits  80

Rulers of the Darkened Room  83

## Chapter 3: Haunted Victorian Storytellers

Edgar Allan Poe  102

Henry James  106

Mark Twain  108

The Brownings  110
Nathaniel Hawthorne  116
Guy de Maupassant  119
Charles Dickens  121

# Chapter 4: A Selection of Shades

The Croglin Vampire  129
The Nurse  139
The Screaming Skeleton  146
The Gray Lady of Hackwood  148
A Ghostly Telegram  152
Quarantined with a Ghost  154
A Devilish Tenant  157
A Spirit Seeks Forgiveness  159
Lady Arabella  161
The Wrotham House Wraith  165
The Monk's Eternal Walk  171

# Chapter 5: Victorian Mysteries

Puzzling Discoveries  179
"Jonah" Bartley  186
The Shades of Jack the Ripper  191
Strange Victorian News  201
Dellschau, Keely and Spear: Inventive Minds  211
Without a Trace  225
Victorian Maritime Mysteries  230

# Acknowledgments

I wish to thank a number of people who have been of tremendous service during the research and writing of this book. I must first mention Janet Bord, of the Fortean Picture Library in Wales, whose generosity and patience made the often frustrating task of tracking down photos an absolute pleasure. Carol Woo, of Ghost House Books, was kind enough to select a few extra images needed to fill in the gaps—thank you as well, Carol.

W. Ritchie Benedict of Calgary, Alberta, was, as always, of invaluable assistance. This book, perhaps more than any other I have written, was substantially shaped by Ritchie's extraordinary research abilities. Ritchie, you have my admiration and appreciation.

The skilled editorial staff at Ghost House Books has always offered me their very best. This time out, I must make special mention of Chris Wangler, whose support and encouragement have been unfailing.

Finally, my thanks and love to the people who support me every day—my friends, family, children and especially my husband, Dennis.

# Introduction

Somehow it has always seemed natural to associate ghosts with Victorian times. Storytellers and movie makers have frequently placed their phantoms in large, rambling 19th-century houses and on narrow, cobbled streets lit dimly by jaundiced gaslight. Perhaps it has been an understandable association—a shady specter simply seems more at home in a Victorian attic than in a modern-day condominium—but perhaps there is more to it than a traditionally creepy atmosphere. When you put the props and lighting effects aside, it is still easy to imagine that something was haunting the people of the era.

Ghosts were certainly a Victorian preoccupation. Any decent overview of Victorian literature must eventually consider Poe, Hawthorne, Maupassant and their counterparts—all considered, to this day, among the finest horror writers to ever put pen to paper. But art is never created in a vacuum; it is always a reflection of the society in which it is created. Apparently, Victorian society had darkness on its mind.

The 19th century was the stage for a tremendous conflict between traditional religion and emerging scientific ideas. Charles Darwin's *The Origin of Species* terrified in a way that no Edgar Allan Poe book ever could—by challenging everything that people had been raised to believe. Great cracks began to show in the religious faith that, until then, had been generally unassailable. A void was being created in people's lives.

One problem of the time was that science, in spite of great advances in numerous areas, was failing to preserve and extend human life. People died at young ages, and they died in vast numbers. They died of diseases, of malnutrition and in tragic accidents. A minor cut could introduce a fatal infection. Childbirth claimed countless young women, whose babies, without benefit of proper infant formula or sterile bottles, often followed them to the grave. Medical treatments were rudimentary at best and harmful at worst; they offered little protection against the ever-looming specter of the reaper. The result was that, amidst the blooming promise of technology, people were still surrounded by and obsessed with death. Victorians raised mourning to an art form that was characterized by strictly observed rules of dress and rigid customs. Such elaborate distractions seemed necessary to mask the anxiety that every person felt when forced to consider that age-old question: what happens to someone after death?

So science had trumped religion, but death still trumped science. As a result, no one felt easy about the afterlife. And *everyone* hoped that there was some scientific way to prove the continued existence of the soul...

Enter spiritualism.

Spiritualism took advantage of the desperate Victorian desire to find some incontrovertible grounds for belief in the afterlife. In séance parlors around the world, levitating tables and disembodied voices seemed to bridge the gap between science and religion. "Here is your proof," said the mediums. "Here is your conclusive evidence." The movement had great momentum, and suddenly people from all walks of life opened their minds to the wildest possibilities.

They were willing to believe that they could communicate with the dead, see the dead, even touch the dead.

In many cases, they were *too* willing to believe. Fraudulent mediums quickly learned how to fake the typical séance phenomena to cash in on their clients' grief and credulity. These tricksters spawned yet another group: scientists who made careers out of exposing them. Still others in the scientific community came together not to advance or discredit, but to investigate paranormal theories objectively. The well-respected Society for Psychical Research was founded in London in 1882, with an American chapter following two years later. Members all had impressive educational backgrounds and moved quickly to set standards of evidence and methods for experimental research.

But it was difficult to impose such a cool-headed approach upon the general public, which embraced the subject in an emotional manner. For every medium of the day who was exposed as a fraud, two more were heralded as miracle workers. For every scholarly essay about the supernatural, there were a dozen newspaper articles breathlessly recounting unfounded personal experiences. And people *wanted* to hear those stories. Ghosts may have been unnerving, but they were also comforting in the sense that they provided proof of an afterlife.

And so it was that the paranormal became a mainstay of Victorian culture. It is little wonder, really, that so many supernatural stories exist from that era and that ghosts and Victoriana seem to go hand in hand.

So, light a candle. Wrap yourself in a blanket. And try to imagine that 19th-century world of shadow, mystery and fear.

# 1
# Famous
# Phantoms

~

*Many of the best-known true ghost stories took place in the Victorian era. They endure because of their drama, their exquisitely unnerving details and the shadowy atmosphere of a time that has long since passed...*

~

# Raynham Hall's Sinister Lady

Raynham Hall is a stately home in Norfolk, England, that serves as the seat of the Marquess of Townshend. No such historic mansion would be complete without a ghost, and Raynham Hall has one with a pedigree—she is believed to be the spirit of Lady Dorothy Townshend, sister of England's first prime minister and wife of Lord Charles Townshend.

Dorothy and Charles had been childhood sweethearts, but, as fate had it, he married another woman and Dorothy became the mistress of the degenerate Lord Wharton. Townshend's wife died at a young age, and Dorothy hastened back to Raynham Hall, determined not to miss her second chance at true love and enormous wealth. She managed to rekindle her old romance and, in 1712, became Lady Dorothy Townshend. All was well for the next decade or so, until Lord Townshend heard whispered stories about his wife's premarital escapades with Wharton. Townshend became enraged and locked Dorothy in her chambers at Raynham Hall. Not long afterward, in 1726, she died. The official cause of death was smallpox, but some said she died of a broken heart. Others suggested that her neck was broken in a mysterious fall down the grand staircase. In any event, Lady Dorothy was gone, but she was determined not to be forgotten. She has been haunting Raynham Hall for nearly three centuries now.

She has always been referred to as the "Brown Lady of Raynham Hall." Until 1904, a portrait of Lady Dorothy wearing a brown brocade gown hung in the hall, and it was in this dress that she always materialized. She was seen and identified by several credible witnesses—not the least of whom was King George IV—but Lady Dorothy made her most chilling appearance shortly after Queen Victoria ascended the throne. The eyewitness on that occasion was Captain Frederick Marryat.

Captain Marryat was a naval hero and the famous author of several rollicking sea adventures. He was one of several guests invited to Raynham Hall to celebrate the redecoration and refurnishing of the mansion. The captain was a boisterous, no-nonsense sort who didn't believe in the supernatural, so the current Lord Townshend felt at ease giving him the room in which Lady Dorothy's portrait hung. There were stories about the portrait itself. It was said that when seen by daylight, it appeared to be a perfectly normal painting, but by flickering candlelight the lady's face took on a skull-like appearance and her eyes seemed to vanish into hollow black sockets. Marryat had heard the stories and declared them to be nonsense, but when he retired that evening, he found himself mesmerized by the strange portrait.

In the likeness, Lady Dorothy's eyes did appear to be exceptionally deep-set. The light of the candle reflected in them, creating a malevolent luminescence.

A sudden pounding on the door startled Captain Marryat out of his unpleasant reverie. When he answered it, he found two young men who had come to seek his technical expertise regarding their firearms. There was to be a shooting party the following day, and they wanted to be well prepared.

*This image of the Brown Lady of Raynham Hall may be the most famous ghost photograph ever taken.*

Captain Marryat, convinced that a few minutes away from the disagreeable portrait would clear his head, offered to go to the young men's room to inspect their guns. That he had already undressed to his undergarments didn't concern him; the other guests had retired to their own rooms hours earlier, and the corridors of the mansion were sure to be deserted. Marryat picked up his own pistol to use for demonstration and told the other fellows to lead the way.

No sooner had the three men set off when they saw a woman approaching from the far end of the dimly lit hall. Embarrassed about his state of undress, Captain Marryat and his companions ducked behind the door of a vacant room. All three watched as the woman drew closer. She was holding a lamp that reflected against the brown silk of her dress and illuminated her gaunt features. Captain Marryat found himself thinking of the repulsive portrait in his room, and his flesh began to creep.

*Surely, this cannot be*, he thought.

At that moment, the woman passed the partially closed door behind which Marryat was hidden. As if in answer to his unspoken question, she turned and looked directly at him in what he later described as a "diabolical manner." Captain Marryat, who had survived 50 naval battles with steady nerves, was so terrified that he unthinkingly raised his pistol and fired point-blank at the profane thing.

The bullet passed cleanly through the apparition. The next morning it was found lodged in the heavy woodwork behind where the ghost had stood.

Although being shot failed to harm the Brown Lady, it may have offended her, since there wasn't another well-publicized spirit sighting at Raynham Hall for close to 90 years. In 1926—200 years after her death—she was seen again by two boys who were playing on the staircase. The youngsters were able to identify the ghost from her portrait, although neither had ever heard the legendary story.

Ten years later, in 1936, Lady Dorothy appeared again and had her photo published in *Country Life* magazine. The image is perhaps the most famous ghost photo in history. Since then, she has been rather elusive.

Though she has not been seen recently, Lady Dorothy Townshend may simply be biding her time. She may have led a short life, but she is enjoying a long afterlife as the sinister Brown Lady of Raynham Hall.

# Willington Mill

A large house, adjacent to a flour mill in Willington Mill, England, was once the site of one of the most persistent hauntings of the 19th century. The strange and frightening activity began in 1834 and continued nearly uninterrupted for approximately 50 years. In that time, the Procter family—who lived there for 13 years beginning in 1834—endured the worst of the phenomena.

It began with thumping and pacing sounds at night that frightened the nursemaid. The disturbance was so great that the woman finally quit and left. By the time a new nursemaid had been hired, the entire family was hearing the noise, which had begun to recur in the daylight hours as well. Often it sounded as though a man in heavy boots was running about on the second floor of the house.

Other mysterious noises included whistling, whizzing and the distinct sound of someone winding a clock. The Procters often heard sticks snapping, hollow drumming and something reminiscent of a bullet striking wood. That alone would have been unsettling.

At night, the beds would tremble and rise up, as if lifted by some invisible force. Members of the family were terrified to feel ice-cold hands pressing down on them. At times, voices either moaned in anguish or spoke short, meaningless phrases. Eventually there were apparitions.

One of the ghosts appeared as a chalky, staring face that hovered at the top of the stairs leading to the attic. The youngest Procter child spoke of a monkey who tugged at his bootstraps and tickled his toes. Another apparition would walk into another child's bedroom, throw open a window, shut it and walk back out again. From outside the house, the Procters and the neighbors frequently saw apparitions in a particular second-story window. One was a luminous priest in a white surplice. Another was a glowing, pale figure of a woman.

It may have been that same spectral woman who presented herself to a curious local physician named Edmund Drury. Drury had heard stories that the house by the mill was haunted, and he asked the Procters' permission to spend a night in it with a friend. The family agreed. On July 3, 1840, Dr. Drury and his companion arrived at the house, armed with pistols and a sense of adventure. They were hoping for some excitement. They got more than they had bargained for. The following is from *Mysteries of the Unknown: Hauntings* (Time-Life Books, 1989):

> At about ten minutes to one in the morning, Drury's eyes "became riveted upon a closet door, which [he]

distinctly saw open, and saw also the figure of a female attired in grayish garments, with the head inclining downwards." The wraith advanced toward him. Screaming, Drury lunged at the figure. But instead of coming to grips with the phantom, he fell on top of his sleeping friend and recollected "nothing distinctly for nearly three hours afterwards." He wrote later, "I have since learned that I was carried downstairs in an agony of fear and terror." Procter noted the next day that Dr. Drury "has got a shock he will not soon cast off."

For several years, John Procter, the father of the family, kept a carefully detailed diary of all the disturbances that took place in his house. It was eventually published in an 1892 edition of the *Journal of the Society for Psychical Research*. Many students of the paranormal found the case fascinating to study. But while they witnessed a wide array of phenomena and kept careful records, no obvious reason for the haunting was ever found and no identification of the troubled spirits was ever made.

The house in Willington Mill was eventually demolished, but its mystery will forever remain intact.

# A Riveting Maritime Tale

Bigger is not always better. At the very least, it is not always luckier. That much was proven by the most famous steamship of the Victorian era—the doomed, iron-hulled liner known as the *Great Eastern*.

The ship was completed in 1857 amid tremendous fanfare. She was five times the size of any vessel of her day, and she was designed to be impressive in every way. But in spite of the high hopes and grand plans, the *Great Eastern* seemed destined for trouble from the very start.

During the ship's construction, five men died. A sixth worker, a riveter, disappeared without giving notice. When the ship was finally launched in London, the huge wave she made when she hit the water sank dozens of small vessels unfortunate enough to be nearby. The people who remained on land fared no better: the gallery that had been built for spectators of the launch collapsed. Hundreds of people were thrown to the ground; many were seriously injured. Eventually, complications from the launch became so costly that the *Great Eastern*'s original owner was bankrupted. It would be more than a year before the ship finally churned out to sea.

When the *Great Eastern* at long last began her sea trials, it was apparent that her luck had not changed. On the ship's very first test voyage, a boiler in the engine room burst. The explosion was said to be so great that most of the glass in the ship shattered. Much worse, however, was the human toll. Five sailors were killed in the explosion, and a sixth drowned when he threw himself overboard to extinguish the flames that had engulfed him. Yet another death followed. When the ship's builder, Isambard Kingdom Brunel, heard the news of the accident, he suffered a serious stroke. Within a month he too was dead.

Finally, on June 17, 1860, the *Great Eastern* set out for New York on her maiden voyage. Her new owners must have agonized over the financial burden of the trip, for while the luxurious liner was designed to accommodate 4000 people comfortably, only 35 had booked passage. Throughout the voyage, those 35 people—and the crew of 418—were bothered by a loud hammering sound that seemed to be coming from the hull. It was particularly noticeable during three frustrating days when the *Great Eastern* bobbed helplessly in the middle of the North Atlantic with her engines silent and her throttles jammed. Eventually, the problem was fixed and the huge ship resumed her course. With the exception of one unpleasant incident involving a cook who went mad and ran around the ship threatening everyone he encountered with a butcher knife, the remainder of the voyage went according to plan. The *Great Eastern* was met with an enthusiastic reception in New York. Between the roar of the crowd and the sickening sound of crunching metal and wood as the gigantic ship ran into the dock, the insistent hammering sounds could barely be heard.

The misfortune that plagued the *Great Eastern* during her construction, launch and maiden voyage stuck with her through her entire career. Despite being one of the first ships designed to carry passengers rather than cargo, she never once sold enough berths to make a profit. She carried her record number of passengers, a mere 1500, in

1862. On that very voyage, the ship drifted slightly off course and through an uncharted area where a sub-merged rock tore a massive gash in her hull. The *Great Eastern*'s double-hulled construction saved her from sinking but nothing, it seemed, could save her from her endless stream of bad luck. The ship was frequently dam-aged in storms and freak mishaps and continued to lose money. By 1863, she had bankrupted her second owners and was purchased by a company who put the ship to work laying trans-Atlantic cable. It was degrading labor for a luxury liner, but she stayed with it for several years. During that time, the humiliated *Great Eastern* suffered fewer mishaps but was still plagued by the incessant pounding in the hull.

By the late 1880s, new ships had been specially designed to lay cable, and the *Great Eastern* had outlived her usefulness. After forcing another set of owners into receivership, she was sold to a salvage firm for the small sum of 16,000 pounds. Even in the scrap yard, however, the huge ship was unpopular. Wrecking crews worked as quickly as they could to dismantle her, claiming that they were constantly disturbed by a loud hammering noise. As they tore apart the immense double hull, the cause of that unremitting pounding, which had afflicted the ship for all of her life, was finally discovered.

There, entombed within the layers of the hull, lay the skeleton of a man. Beside him was a bag of rusted tools. It was the riveter who had gone missing when the ship was being built.

And so, in the final days of the *Great Eastern*'s existence, the cause of her perpetual misfortune was discovered. She had been haunted by the spirit of the terrified worker who had been sealed alive inside the hull. Carrying such a cursed cargo, it is little wonder that the famous ship never spent an easy day at sea.

# The Greenbrier Ghost

In the fall of 1896, in the town of Greenbrier, West Virginia, a woman named Mary Jane Heaster was facing a problem common to mothers everywhere: her daughter Zona was involved with an unsuitable man.

"There's something about him I don't like, Zona," she often said. "Something I can't quite put my finger on."

Zona would always laugh at her mother's concerns.

"Oh, Mama," she would scoff, "it's just that you haven't known him all your life, like everyone else around here."

Mary Jane was the first to admit that she was suspicious of strangers. She didn't understand why Zona couldn't have found herself a nice local man.

"Now where's the excitement in that?" was Zona's typical response.

Zona and her suitor, an itinerant blacksmith named Edward Shue, had only known each other for a few weeks when they married on October 26, 1896. Mary Jane Heaster attended the small ceremony with her mouth set in a grim line. She had not warmed to Edward Shue at all, and her intuition was telling her that no good would come of the union.

"Mark my words," she confided to a friend, "this is going to end badly for Zona."

Mary Jane was right; she just had no idea exactly how badly or how soon the marriage would end. As it happened, Zona had not even been wed a full three months when an errand boy found her lying dead on her kitchen floor.

Edward Shue was notified immediately and went racing home. When the coroner arrived, about an hour later, he found Edward in a nearly hysterical state of grief. He had carried his wife's body up to the bedroom and changed her into her finest dress—one with a high, stiff collar and a large bow at the neck. A black net veil covered her face. All through the coroner's examination, Edward Shue remained bent over Zona's upper body, cradling her head and sobbing uncontrollably. His grief was so severe that the coroner was forced to conduct the most superficial of examinations. When he could find no obvious cause of death, he pronounced that Zona had died of "an everlasting faint" and left Edward Shue to mourn his loss in private.

At Zona's wake, Edward Shue remained inconsolable. He had placed pillows on either side of his dead wife's head, so that she might rest more comfortably. He had wrapped a voluminous scarf around her neck, claiming that it had been her favorite and that she had wished to be buried in it. And he hovered protectively over Zona's body, throwing himself across the head of the coffin whenever anyone came near. There was a moment, however, as the body was being moved to the cemetery, when people got a good look at the strange way Zona's head lolled about. That, along with Edward Shue's fanatical behavior, started people whispering.

Some people were suspicious of Shue, but none more so than Mary Jane Heaster. While Mary Jane mourned her daughter's death, she also prayed that the young woman's spirit would visit her and explain exactly how she had met her end. It was not long before her prayers were answered. One night, several weeks after the wake, Mary Jane awoke to see a glowing figure standing next to her bed. It was Zona's ghost, eager to share the details of her murder.

"Mama, you were right about Edward," the apparition lamented. "He was cruel to me, very cruel." Zona's spirit explained that on the last day of her life, Edward had attacked her in a fit of rage because she had failed to prepare a meal for him. He had broken her neck, she said. Mary Jane watched in horror as the wraith of her daughter illustrated her point by turning her head a full 360 degrees.

For four consecutive nights, Mary Jane was awakened by Zona's ghost. Four times, she heard the sad and gruesome details of her daughter's death. And four times the spirit pleaded with her to not let the murderer go free. Mary Jane Heaster vowed that she would not allow that to happen. On the morning of the fifth day, she paid a visit to the authorities.

The local prosecutor, a man named John Preston, may not have believed Mary Jane's tales of visits from beyond the grave. But there had been much local gossip about Zona Shue's untimely death, and he probably didn't need much convincing that the matter was worthy of investigation. Preston ordered that Zona's body be exhumed and a proper autopsy be performed. The results showed that the young woman had a crushed windpipe and a broken neck. She had not succumbed to "an everlasting faint" but had been brutally murdered. Edward Shue, who had acted so strangely and gone to such extremes to prevent a coroner's proper examination, was promptly arrested for the crime.

"They will never be able to prove that I did it," Shue kept saying. And it was true that much of the evidence against him was circumstantial. But what Edward Shue wasn't counting on was that the trial jury would hear a full account of the murder as it had been described by the victim herself.

The prosecution was not able to present Mary Jane Heaster's ghost story as evidence, because it fell into the category of hearsay. Ironically, it was the defense council who raised the subject during cross-examination, probably in the hopes of discrediting Mary Jane. The plan backfired, however, when Mary Jane won the jury over with a vivid description of her dead daughter's visits. The jury deliberated only briefly before finding Edward Shue guilty of his wife's murder.

Shue was sentenced to life imprisonment and died in West Virginia's state penitentiary. As for Zona, she is memorialized in a highway historical marker near Greenbrier that tells her story:

> Interred in a nearby cemetery is Zona Heaster Shue. Her death in 1897 was presumed natural until her spirit appeared to her mother to describe how she was killed by her husband Edward. Autopsy on the

exhumed body verified the apparition's account. Edward, found guilty of murder, was sentenced to the state prison. Only known case in which testimony from ghost helped convict a murderer.

# An Adventure at Versailles

In the summer of 1901, two English scholars named Anne Moberly and Eleanor Jourdain traveled to Paris on vacation. The two women had known each other only a short time, but they were of similar dispositions and had much in common. They were both very traditional, conservative ladies who addressed each other as "Miss Moberly" and "Miss Jourdain." Both had been raised in clerical households; Moberly was the daughter of an Anglican bishop and Jourdain's father was a vicar. And both shared similar academic backgrounds. There was nothing in their proper pasts that could have prepared the women for the unique experience that they were about to share.

On the morning of August 10, the traveling companions went by train from Paris to Versailles. Neither Moberly nor Jourdain was well versed in French history, but both wanted to see the famed Palace of Versailles and the Petit Trianon, which was known to have been a favorite retreat of the doomed queen Marie Antoinette. The two women toured the palace, then set out on a long walk toward the Petit Trianon.

It was a fresh, breezy day. The friends enjoyed the scenery of the gardens and the pleasure of one another's company. They might have paid more attention to their guidebook, however, since at one point they found themselves lost. Moberly and Jourdain emerged from a glade to find themselves not at the Petit Trianon, but at the *Grand* Trianon. After consulting their map, they set off in another direction. As they passed one particular building, Moberly saw a woman lean out a window to shake the dust out of a tablecloth. Moberly expected that Eleanor Jourdain, the only one of the pair who was fluent in French, would ask her to confirm their directions. Curiously, though, the normally outgoing Jourdain completely ignored the woman. Anne Moberly made no mention of it, and the two continued on their way.

The grounds had become curiously deserted, but at a point where the path branched off in several directions, the friends came upon two men wearing grayish-green coats and small, tricornered hats. Eleanor Jourdain asked them which of the paths led to the Petit Trianon. One of the men answered, but in such a cold, robotic fashion that both women were quite unnerved by the exchange. They started down the path the man had indicated, past a cottage where Jourdain noticed a woman and young girl in old-fashioned attire standing in the doorway.

At that point in their journey, both Moberly and Jourdain found themselves battling a sudden and unexplainable depression. Neither woman said anything about her abrupt change in mood; instead, both struggled silently against the unexpected onslaught of loneliness and gloom. They walked on, toward the Petit Trianon, but the lovely summer day had lost its luster. Even the natural beauty of the woods appeared to be somehow suppressed. Moberly later wrote that her surroundings "suddenly looked unnatural, therefore unpleasant; even the trees...seemed to have become flat and lifeless, like a wood worked in tapestry. There were no effects of light and shade, and no wind stirred the trees. It was all intensely still."

In this peculiar atmosphere, the friends arrived at another place where the path diverged. Set amongst the trees, directly ahead of the women, was a small, round kiosk. A cloaked man sat there, his back turned to the path. As Moberly and Jourdain approached, the air seemed to grow increasingly heavy and motionless. The women both felt intense dread, which escalated into near panic when the man turned around to look at them. There was something in his cruel, pockmarked face that both frightened and repulsed them. As luck would have it, though, the women were not forced to ask the ominous stranger to assist them with directions. At the moment they reached the fork, a handsome man with long, black curls and an 18th-century costume came running up behind them. Before Jourdain could pose the question, he called out that the path to the right would lead them to the Petit Trianon. Then, before the two friends could thank the man, he was gone.

Moberly and Jourdain turned to the right and hurried along, eager to distance themselves from the vile, cloaked man at the kiosk. They walked for some time through a dark wood. When they finally emerged, they were rewarded with their first view of the Petit Trianon. It was an elegant structure, flanked on two sides by a broad terrace and surrounded by lovely, English-style gardens.

The women walked toward the royal residence, still feeling oddly subdued. Moberly felt as though she was in a dreamlike state as she passed a woman who was sketching near the edge of the terrace. The woman was wearing an elaborate, old-fashioned outfit that was quite inappropriate for a day of sightseeing. It caught Anne Moberly's attention, but she said nothing of it to Eleanor Jourdain.

The two women made their way around to a courtyard along the south side of the palace. There, they found a lively crowd of tourists, all dressed in modern fashions. Moberly and Jourdain tagged along with the group and felt their spirits lift as they went on a tour of the historic building. By the time they left the Petit Trianon, the world had resumed its natural appearance and Moberly and Jourdain had regained their former good spirits. As they left Versailles, neither woman had any intention of mentioning what an odd experience it had been.

And so it was for a week, until Anne Moberly sat down to write to her sister about the details of the trip. As she attempted to describe the day in Versailles, she felt the same dark mood descend upon her again. Impulsively, she turned to Eleanor Jourdain and said, "Do you think that the Petit Trianon is haunted?"

Without pausing to think, Jourdain replied, "Yes, I do."

For the first time, the two women compared their experiences and were astounded by the similarities and differences. Both had been plagued by the inexplicable depression and had sensed an altering of the landscape and atmosphere. Both had been unsettled by the men in the grayish-green coats and frightened by the dark, cloaked character who sat in the kiosk in the woods. But

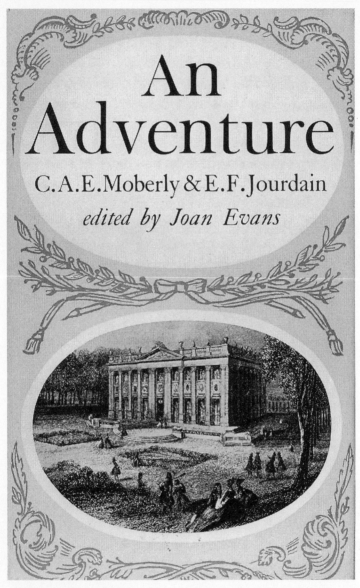

*A 1955 edition of the famous book written by Anne Moberly and Eleanor Jourdain*

Jourdain was mystified by Anne Moberly's description of the woman with the sketch pad. She recalled the garden and terrace to the north of the Petit Trianon being absolutely deserted. She had also been unaware of the woman shaking out the cloth. Likewise, Moberly had no recollection of the cottage in the woods or of the woman and girl in period costume. The longer they talked, the more convinced the women were that they had shared some strange supernatural experience that had provided them each with a slightly different view of the past. They resolved to revisit Versailles and research its history in an attempt to understand what they had witnessed.

On return trips to the historic site, Moberly and Jourdain discovered that there was no kiosk or cottage along the path. A study of architectural documents confirmed that those structures had existed more than 120 years prior to their initial visit. Moberly was stunned to see that there was a large shrub marking the exact spot near the Petit Trianon's terrace where she had seen the woman sketching. She was even more shocked when she was shown a portrait of Marie Antoinette and recognized her to be that woman. After more research, the women were convinced that the men in the grayish-green coats and tricorne hats had been members of the Swiss Guard, and that the malevolent cloaked man had been the Comte de Vaudreuil, a traitor to the royal family. Perhaps the most convincing piece of evidence was a significant date that the two women discovered: it was on August 10, 1792, that revolutionary forces had arrested the royal family. It was on August 10, 1901—the 109th anniversary of that dark, historic day—when

Anne Moberly and Eleanor Jourdain first visited the tragic queen's beloved home.

Ten years after the amazing event, Moberly and Jourdain published a book detailing their experience. Entitled *An Adventure*, it went on to sell very well and inspire great debate about the authenticity of the authors' story. There were many—including members of the Society for Psychical Research—who were critical of the women's research and doubted its veracity. Still others suspected that Moberly and Jourdain had simply encountered actors in period costume who had gathered to rehearse a play. Even those who believed the tale have always had questions: did the women experience an extended episode of retrocognition, or did they travel back in time? The truth may never be known. All anyone can be certain of is that, on that lovely August day, Anne Moberly and Eleanor Jourdain shared something truly remarkable. Whether it was a misconception or a paranormal experience, it will always be remembered as an adventure.

# Number 50, Berkeley Square

In May 1879, *Mayfair* magazine ran an article featuring what was reputed to be "the most haunted house in London." It was a fashionable West End address, number 50, Berkeley Square.

At the time, the neighbors had been complaining about the house for years. At best, it was in a terrible state of disrepair—an eyesore in their well-to-do community. At worst, it was the source of terrifying loud noises and unsettling phenomena that included self-propelled furnishings and windows that would fly open and spew objects ranging from books to stones. The house had an unsavory reputation that had been decades in the making. In the 1830s, a young woman had reportedly thrown herself from an upstairs window to escape the sexual advances of her uncle. Years later, a man named Myers bought and furnished the house to please his fiancée, who then jilted him for another man. The rejection caused Myers to lose his sanity. By day, he secluded himself in a tiny garret room. By night, he wandered through the deserted rooms of his mansion holding a flickering candle and mourning the loss of his one true love. After he died, it was said that the spirit of "Mad Myers" lingered, joining the specter of the girl who had fallen to her death. So the house had long been reputed to be haunted, but no one knew exactly *how* haunted until a family by the name of Bentley moved into the house and inherited its unholy ambience.

One night in 1880, a maid who worked for the Bentleys was preparing one of the guest rooms for the fiancé of the eldest daughter. Suddenly the maid began to scream. Everyone in the house rushed to her aid, but they were not quick enough. By the time they reached the room, the poor woman was writhing on the floor with her facial features twisted into a mask of stark terror. She was rushed to the hospital but died the following day.

The Bentleys' daughter, fearing that the ghost stories were true after all, begged that her fiancé be given a different room in which to stay. The young man, an army officer named Captain Kentfield, scoffed at the notion. In fact, he insisted on sleeping in the room where the maid had gone mad. He told his betrothed not to worry and promised that after he had settled in, he would ring the service bell once to signal the family that he was well. He said that he would ring more than once in the unlikely event that he needed someone's assistance.

Captain Kentfield retired to his room. His fiancée waited nervously for his signal and was greatly relieved when she heard a single ring of the service bell. After only a few minutes had passed, however, the bell rang again—and again and again and again. The frantic noise stopped mere seconds before the girl and her family burst into the room. There, they discovered Captain Kentfield in the middle of the floor, curled into a fetal position with his mouth gaping open in a silent scream. His eyes were fixed on an empty corner of the room. Whatever it was he had seen there had literally frightened him to death.

The Bentleys weren't willing to risk staying in a house that killed, no matter how lovely the neighborhood. They quickly arranged other accommodations for themselves and left number 50, Berkeley Square. Once again, the house sat empty and cold, void of human company. So it stayed until December 24, 1887.

Two sailors from the frigate HMS *Penelope* were in London on that Christmas Eve, looking for a place to stay. They happened to walk past the old house in Berkeley Square and noticed that someone had put a sign on the front door saying that the property was available to let. There was no one home to answer the door, however, so the sailors let themselves in, thinking that they would locate their new landlord and pay the rent at the earliest opportunity. That opportunity never arrived because the men chose to sleep in the second-story bedroom that had claimed at least two other lives.

In the middle of the night, they heard dragging footsteps in the hall. Suddenly the door swung open on rusty hinges.

On Christmas morning, the neighbors awoke to see one of the sailors impaled on the railings alongside the basement steps. He appeared to have fallen out of one of the second-story windows to his gruesome death. The nearby hospital was dealing with the second sailor, now a wild-eyed lunatic raving about having been attacked in a deserted house by a monstrous, black shapeless thing. Or perhaps the attacker had been a tall, white-faced ghoul with a slack, gaping maw. Or perhaps...

Which *was* it?

The truth of the matter is, there are several versions of the story associated with number 50, Berkeley Square. The maid is sometimes found dead, other times found raving mad and only able to utter the words "I have seen it." The young man is sometimes killed and other times is left to recover from his fright but will "never be the same again." His name is variously Captain Kentfield, Captain Raymond or Sir Robert Warboys. In the Warboys version, he is not visiting his fiancée, but staying in the room to win a dare. Sometimes, there is a pistol shot heard before the family can reach the bedroom. One version has it that the young man has fired a shot into the wall, and another has it that he has turned the gun on himself. The sailors are sometimes attacked in the cursed bedroom, and sometimes they encounter a murderous ghost or creature while investigating strange noises in the house. With so many differing accounts of the same story, can *any* of them be true?

It's difficult to say. The number of variations may indicate that the tale is pure folklore, invented to complement the image of a neglected, run-down mansion. But others say that where there's smoke, there's fire—meaning that where so many spooky tales have evolved, there's surely some grain of ghostly truth. Either way—fact or fiction—number 50, Berkeley Square remains the most famously haunted address of Victorian-era London.

# A Horror in Amherst

No one ever thought of 19-year-old Esther Cox as a particularly pretty or appealing girl. She was often described as stout, plain, moody and unpleasantly sulky. She had only the most basic education and little knowledge of the world beyond her small hometown of Amherst, Nova Scotia. But a young man named Bob McNeal, who was considered handsome and charming, if a bit of a wild card, obviously found something that he liked about the girl. It may have been nothing more than her absolute availability, but it inspired McNeal to ask Esther out for a buggy ride with him. She accepted.

The outing was set for August 28, 1878—a date that has ever since been associated with the onset of one of the most famous and violent hauntings in Canadian history.

Esther lived with her large, extended family in the home of her sister and brother-in-law, Olive and Daniel Teed. When Bob McNeal drove up to the Teeds' rented, two-story clapboard house on the evening of August 28, the sky was threatening rain. McNeal insisted that he and Esther not change their plans, however. He showed her that the open buggy had a top that could be raised in the event of a shower. He made every effort to be charming and convincing and, in the end, Esther agreed that she would still go. As the young couple rode off down the street, Esther glanced nervously at the darkening horizon and worried about soaking her best dress. Within an hour, she would learn that her new suitor was far more threatening than the gathering storm clouds.

McNeal drove the buggy out of town and down a winding dirt road that cut through the heart of a dark forest. When he had gone some distance into the woods, he stopped his horse and turned to Esther. His intense blue eyes betrayed an inner turbulence far more extreme than the weather.

"I want you to come into the woods with me," he said.

Esther gaped at him.

"I will *not*," she replied. Esther had not had many suitors, but she was worldly enough to know what McNeal was suggesting. She also knew that no young woman of decent character would accept such a proposition. "Turn this buggy around," she demanded. "I want to go home this minute!"

McNeal made no move to pick up the reins. Instead, he reached into his coat pocket and produced a large pistol. With a shaking hand, he aimed it at Esther.

"Get out," he told her. "Do as I say. We're going into those woods."

"Don't be foolish," Esther whispered. "Put that away, before—"

But McNeal would not listen. He swore loudly at Esther and grabbed her roughly by the arm. He tried to force her from the buggy, but she struggled against him. Thunder rumbled overhead, and fat raindrops began to fall. A brilliant bolt of lightning split a nearby tree with a deafening crack. Then, as the howling wind let up for a moment, another sound could be heard—a sound that was distant, but growing nearer.

"Do you hear that!" cried Esther. "Someone's coming!"

McNeal paused, panting. Within seconds, even through the pouring rain, he could make out the distinctive sound of wagon wheels rumbling in the distance.

"Damnation!"

McNeal threw Esther violently against the seat of the buggy and put away his pistol. He let loose a stream of vulgar profanity as he grabbed the reins and jerked them, urging his horse to turn around.

A few minutes later, two men driving a heavy wagon pulled over to the shoulder of the narrow road to allow Bob McNeal's buggy to pass. The driver of the wagon raised his eyebrows as McNeal sped past, apparently giving no thought to the weather conditions or the fact that he was crowding the other rig.

"Hell of a hurry!" he complained to his friend.

"Aye," said the friend. "He couldn't even take the time to stop and put up the top for his poor missus!"

Esther arrived home safely, but she was drenched to the bone and utterly humiliated by what had happened. Bob McNeal all but threw her out of the buggy when they reached the Teed family's front door, then raced off into the night. Esther let herself into the house and crept upstairs to the room that she shared with her sister, Jane. She changed out of her sodden clothing and crawled gratefully beneath the covers of the lumpy bed. She was careful to weep very quietly, so as not to wake her sister.

For the next four days, Esther's family cut a wide swath around her. Red-eyed and ill-tempered, the girl was prone to fits of tears. Everyone assumed that her time with Bob McNeal had not gone well, but no one dared to ask. Then, on the evening of the fourth day, a series of events began to divert attention from all other problems.

Esther and Jane were settled into bed and had just begun to drift off to sleep. Suddenly Esther screamed and jumped out from under the covers.

"There's a mouse!" she shrieked. "There's a mouse in the blankets! I felt it crawling about me!"

Jane got out of bed and lit a lamp. Together, the girls took apart the bedding and searched each of the covers. No mouse could be found. But as they were making the bed up again, Jane noticed a stealthy, snake-like movement within the mattress itself.

"Esther, look," she said. "If that's a mouse, it can't touch us. It's trapped in the straw, beneath the ticking."

The girls returned wearily to bed. They pulled up the covers and went to sleep. It was the last relatively uneventful night that they would enjoy for a very long time.

The next evening, everyone in the household was awakened by Esther's and Jane's shrieking. When Daniel Teed burst through the door of their small bedroom, he found both of his sisters-in-law crouched on the floor, staring at a disorderly pile of cotton quilting squares.

"What is it?" he demanded.

"We heard scratching," Esther sobbed.

"We thought the mouse had gotten into our box of squares," Jane added.

"You woke me for a *mouse?*" Daniel said.

The sisters shook their heads and pointed to the far corner of the room. Daniel turned and gasped. There, suspended in mid-air, was the box that was used to store scraps of cloth. It dipped and swayed and lazily turned upside down. A few remaining pieces of fabric fell out of the box and fluttered to the floor. By the time the night was over, everyone in the house had marveled over the way the box jumped and flew around the room of its own accord. When the phenomenon finally ended, they imagined that they would never see the likes of it again. They were wrong.

The very next night, Jane was wrenched out of a deep sleep by Esther's bloodcurdling scream.

"My God! What's the matter with me? I'm dying!" she wailed. "I'm swelling up and shall certainly burst, I know I shall!"

Jane quickly lit a lamp with a shaking hand and was horrified by what she saw. Esther's hair seemed to be standing on end, and her eyes were bulging. The girl's skin was blood red and burning hot to the touch. She writhed, gnashed her teeth wildly and cried out in pain. Then, as Daniel Teed entered the room to see what the commotion was, Esther began to swell. While her color went from red to ghastly white and back again, her body ballooned to nearly twice its normal size. The girl screamed in pain as her skin stretched to beyond capacity.

"She's going to burst! She's going to die!" cried Olive Teed when she entered the room and saw her younger sister. But at that moment, three thunderous bangs sounded from beneath the bed, and Esther deflated as though she had been punctured. Her fever subsided and she fell into a fitful sleep.

In the morning, Daniel Teed went to fetch the doctor, a man by the name of Thomas Carritte. Dr. Carritte informed Teed that he believed none of his foolish story but would attend to Esther anyway. At the very moment the physician walked into the girl's bedroom, however, he changed his mind. There, he watched in amazement as Esther's pillow slid back and forth beneath her head and bursts of noise came from the empty space beneath the bed. Before Dr. Carritte could even examine his patient, the angry spirit made it clear that he would be powerless to treat her. The bedclothes lifted up and flew across the room, then a loud scratching sound came from the wall above Esther's head. The doctor could see that letters, each one nearly a foot high, were being carved into the plaster as if by some invisible hand. Within minutes, the cruel message was complete. It read:

ESTHER COX, YOU ARE MINE TO KILL

Once the words had been written, a large chunk of plaster tore itself loose from the wall and hurtled across the room toward the doctor. As it landed at his feet, a terrible pounding noise began. This noise went on for hours; even as Dr. Carritte left the Teeds' home that night he could hear it. When he returned the next evening with a strong sedative for Esther, the noises had ended. But Dr. Carritte was to witness an entirely new phenomenon. As he bent over his patient to examine her on that occasion, a torrent of potatoes appeared out of thin air and pelted him from across the room. It was apparent that the doctor was powerless to rid Esther Cox of her poltergeist.

Perhaps the presence understood, because it became even more bold and destructive. Lit matches would frequently materialize in mid-air and drop on the furnishings or people's clothing. Knives and forks would whiz through the air and embed themselves in the walls. Chairs were often flipped over as easily as if they had been made of tissue paper, and huge, heavy objects would float about the house like clouds. Numerous visitors, such as Dr. Carritte, were subjected to the phenomena. One man came within scant inches of being injured when a large glass paperweight flew across the room and struck the sofa beside his head. A young neighbor's pocketknife was wrenched from his hands and stabbed into Esther's back. Even the family's Methodist minister, Reverend Temple, bore witness to the evil chaos. Once, as he sat at the Teeds' kitchen table, the minister was horrified to see a bucket of cold drinking water, which had been set on the table, come to a full and furious boil.

The haunting continued for months on end. On several occasions, Daniel Teed arranged to have Esther live elsewhere, hoping that his sister-in-law's absence would bring an end to the dreadful situation. Sending the girl away never proved to be a permanent solution, however. On one occasion, when all seemed to be going well, Olive and Jane begged Daniel to allow their sister to return home. Other times, people who had been allowing Esther to board with them would send her back to the Teeds, claiming that the poltergeist had begun to terrorize their own homes. Even people for whom the girl worked suffered by association. A man named John White hired Esther to work in his restaurant but was forced to let her go because of the disturbance she caused. The furniture had started to move around the dining room on its own, there were incessant rapping noises throughout the building and a huge oven door refused to stay properly shut on days when the poor girl was working.

Eventually, Esther found another job working on a farm that belonged to a man named Arthur Davison, who was the county clerk. She had only been there a short time before the spirit began to act up. First, a number of things belonging to the family with whom she had last stayed appeared as if by magic in Davison's barn. Esther was quickly accused of theft. Before anything could be proven, the barn caught fire and burned to the ground. Esther said that it had been the work of the nasty poltergeist, which seemed to be a convenient excuse given that she had been the last person seen near the building. In the end, a judge who did not believe in supernatural foolishness convicted Esther Cox of arson. She was sentenced to spend four months in prison.

Ironically, this low point also proved to be a turning point for Esther. She was released from prison early, met a fellow from the nearby town of Springhill and got married. At last, as she settled into married domesticity, Esther Cox was rid of the poltergeist that had plagued her for more than a year. By all accounts she enjoyed a relatively quiet and normal existence for the remainder of her life.

More than a century has passed since the events of the Amherst haunting, but people are still fascinated with the case. Every generation brings with it a new crop of psychical researchers who are eager to examine the evidence and determine the cause of what happened. Though it remains a mystery, careful study of the facts has produced a number of popular theories.

First among them is the belief that Esther created the disturbances herself. She was an unpopular, hysterical, antisocial sort of person who may have gone to extreme measures to gain attention. Many believed her to be capable of fraud. Still, it is almost impossible to imagine that the girl who was described by most as being not terribly bright could have masterminded the kinds of manifestations that left educated people baffled.

The second and perhaps most widely accepted opinion is that the Amherst situation was a classic example of a poltergeist. In *The Encyclopedia of Ghosts and Spirits* (Facts on File, 1992), author Rosemary Ellen Guiley explained it as follows:

> ...it is likely that Esther was the unwitting focus of psychokinetic energy, which caused the phenomena, due to repressed emotions. She was within the age range of common poltergeist disturbances believed to be caused by human agents. She may have suffered repressed  hostility and tension, perhaps from living in very close quarters with a large family. She also may have suffered repressed sexual feelings.

The release of such frustration and anger could explain why the phenomena began immediately following Bob McNeal's attempt to rape Esther. But there is one other way to analyze the case that also involves McNeal. After the evening of August 28, 1878, Bob McNeal was not seen in Amherst again. He might have simply run away, fearing that he would be punished for his actions, but it is also quite feasible that he may have gone to some secluded place and turned his pistol on himself. If so, he might have been the ghost who tormented Esther, having found a way to control her in death that he had not found in life. It is interesting to note that, for a time, Esther and her family were able to communicate with the entities that plagued them. In those communications, they were informed that there were actually three spirits and that the most violent and destructive of all of them was named "Bob Nickel"—a name not far removed from "Bob McNeal." Could they have been one and the same? Could Esther's disturbed suitor have returned from the grave to torment her?

No one knows and no one will ever know. Those dramatic events that took place in Amherst so long ago are destined to forever remain a mystery.

# Ballechin House

In February 1897, the Society for Psychical Research sent two of its most trusted investigators to stay in a rambling old home in the remote, snowy Scottish Highlands. They had no problem securing a lease on the place, though it was a desirable country estate with extensive grounds. The house was conveniently vacant because previous tenants, who had paid a full year's rent in advance, had fled after only seven weeks without bothering to ask for a refund.

That was just the sort of effect that Ballechin House had on people. It was the way it had been ever since a previous owner, Major Robert Steuart, had died and was denied his means of returning to this earth.

Ballechin House was built in 1806 on the Steuart family estate. In 1850, it was inherited by "the Major," as he preferred to be addressed. Steuart was a retired officer of the East India Company and an eccentric in every sense of the word. He had returned from India some years before, sporting a pronounced limp and a firm belief in the transmigration of souls. He would tell anyone who would listen that after his death he planned to return to earth in the body of his favorite dog, a large black spaniel. Perhaps to hedge his bets, the Major kept a total of 14 pampered dogs in the house, each one ready to receive his soul at a moment's notice.

In 1876, Major Robert Steuart died. Whether or not he successfully transmigrated will never be known, because the nephew who inherited Ballechin House— a man by the name of John Steuart—had no intention of cohabiting with the canine reincarnation of his peculiar uncle. His first act as the new master of the house was to shoot all 14 of the Major's beloved hounds, beginning with the black spaniel.

That was when the haunting—likely a ghostly expression of outrage—began.

John Steuart's wife was the first to realize that Ballechin House had not been thoroughly vacated for their family. She was working on the household accounts one afternoon when the room she was in suddenly filled with the distinct and powerful scent of dogs. No sooner had Mrs. Steuart noticed this than she felt something unseen rub up against her leg. It was a sensation she had experienced many times before. She knew that she had just been touched by the body of a large, invisible dog. Other phenomena followed soon thereafter. Frightening sounds disturbed the family's sleep, and disturbing images often appeared and then vanished. In what had once been the Major's bedroom, the Steuarts frequently heard the loud, uneven footfalls of someone who walked with a pronounced limp. Guests who came to stay would often inquire at breakfast about the angry, indistinguishable voices that had awakened them. It was abundantly clear that since the Major's death, Ballechin House had become quite haunted.

The Steuart family had difficulty keeping servants, but they coped quite well otherwise. By building a new, unhaunted wing for the children to sleep in, they managed to live in their ancestral home for 21 years.

In 1897, John Steuart died, and Ballechin House passed into the hands of an heir who had no desire to live in it. The man began renting the house to others—but found that tenants were unwilling to spend much time in a house where apparitions wandered the halls and the bedclothes were pulled off by invisible hands. Then, just when it appeared that Ballechin House was destined to sit empty, the two investigators from the Society for Psychical Research signed a lease. Colonel Lemesurier Taylor and Ada Goodrich Freer moved in on a snowy February day, hoping for the worst.

Ballechin House did not disappoint.

Freer later wrote that her first impression upon seeing the house was that it "looked very gloomy." Inside, she noted that it "felt like a vault." Apparently, the house didn't care much for Freer either, for it awakened her on that very first night with a deafening clanging noise. It was the beginning of a nearly nonstop stream of ghostly phenomena that Freer and Taylor carefully documented.

The investigators—and additional guests who were invited as unwitting participants in the experiment—experienced all that the Steuart family had been subjected to, and more. They often heard disembodied voices, including that of a priest who was regularly heard reciting his divine office. Apparitions included the figure of a nun and the upper half of a woman in a shawl who seemed to be suspended in mid-air. Some people, including Freer, reported being touched by unseen hands. The invisible specter of the Major continued to limp around his bedroom for the new guests, and his cherished pets remained in the house as well. One night, Ada Goodrich Freer was awakened by the whimpering of her own little Pomeranian. When she turned on a light, she saw two large, black paws resting on the table beside her bed. The image faded away long before the "sickening sensation" in Freer's stomach did.

After 69 days in Ballechin House, Taylor and Freer felt that they had more than enough information. They concluded that at least nine different spirits occupied the house and grounds. But the Steuart family was outraged to discover that such an experiment had taken place and threatened legal action if the story was made public. Taylor and Freer still published their findings in an 1899 book, but they changed all names and were cautiously vague about other identifying information. As a result, *The Alleged Haunting of B— House* was never taken particularly seriously by other paranormal researchers.

As for Ballechin House itself, it was torn down in 1963. No one seems to know whether or not the Major kept limping around his bedroom into the 20th century. Perhaps he, and all the other spirits who haunted "B— House," finally transmigrated to some other, more welcoming plane of existence.

# "The Morton Case"

In 1882, a young woman named Rosina Despard lived with her family in a lovely three-story house on Pittville Circus Road in Cheltenham, England. The Despards had only lived in the house for a few months when Rosina witnessed something decidedly unusual. Rather than mention it to her family, she wrote of her experience in a letter to a friend. This correspondence was the first of several detailed accounts written by Rosina that were destined to become evidence in one of the most famous paranormal investigations of all time. It began:

> I had gone up to my room, but was not yet in bed, when I heard someone at the door, and went to it, thinking it might be my mother. On opening the door, I saw no one; but on going a few steps along the passage, I saw the figure of a tall lady, dressed in black, standing at the head of the stairs. After a few moments she descended the stairs, and I followed for a short distance, feeling curious what it could be. I had only a small piece of candle, and it suddenly burnt itself out; and being unable to see more, I went back to my room.

> The figure was that of a tall lady, dressed in black of a soft woolen material, judging from the slight sound in moving. The face was hidden in a handkerchief held in the right hand. This is all I noticed then; but on further occasions, when I was able to observe her

more closely, I saw the upper part of the left side of the forehead, and a little more of the hair above. Her left hand was nearly hidden by her sleeve and a fold of her dress. As she held it down a portion of a widow's cuff was visible on both wrists, so that the whole impression was that of a lady in widow's weeds. There was no cap on the head, but a general effect of blackness suggests a bonnet, with a long veil or a hood.

Rosina was convinced that the woman in black was a ghost. During the first two years that the Despards lived in the house, Rosina saw her at least six times. The apparition often followed the same path—she would pass down the stairs, pause in front of the bay window and then move down the hall toward the garden door, where she would vanish. On at least one remarkable occasion, she appeared to Rosina in the living room, in front of several other members of the Despard family. Again, Rosina said nothing, although she admitted that she had been "astonished that no one else in the room saw her..." The ghost stood behind the couch in the living room for approximately half an hour. Then she left, moving down the hall toward the garden door as she had on previous occasions.

Rosina continued to keep careful records in the form of letters to her friend, but she said nothing to her family until the summer of 1884. It was then that she discovered she had not been the only person to see the woman in black. Others had encountered her as well—but had been convinced that the phantom was a flesh-and-blood person. Rosina's married sister had once mistaken the

*The house on Pittville Circus Road, once the scene of a famous haunting, has long since been converted to flats.*

mourning specter for a visiting nun. A maid had seen her and feared that someone had broken into the house. Even Rosina's younger brother, along with a playmate, had observed the woman weeping as she gazed out the bay window at them. The two boys ran in the house to see who it was that was so upset, but they found the living room to be quite empty.

In August 1884, the apparition of the woman in black began to be seen more frequently, and by more people. On one particular evening, four different people encountered her, the first being Rosina's sister Edith, who had been singing in the drawing room. Rosina wrote:

> She said she had seen the figure in the drawing-room, close behind her as she sat at the piano. I went back into the room with her, and saw the figure in the bow window in her usual place. I spoke to her several times, but had no answer. She stood there for about 10 minutes or a quarter of an hour; then went across the room to the door, and along the passage, disappearing in the same place by the garden door.

> My sister M[abel] then came in from the garden, saying that she had seen her coming up the kitchen steps outside. We all three then went out into the garden, when Mrs. K[inloch] called out from a window in the first story that she had just seen her pass across the lawn in front, and along the carriage drive towards the orchard.

The sightings continued, and Rosina continued to keep thorough notes. By December 1884, she had contacted Frederic Myers, of the Society for Psychical Research, to see if he would be interested in investigating the case. Myers visited the Despards in early 1885 and found them to be completely credible. He began to interview the principal witnesses and encouraged Rosina to attempt certain experiments whenever she found herself in the presence of the ghost. At Myers' suggestion, Rosina kept a camera close at hand, though she failed to ever capture the ghost on film. She also made a habit of tying threads across the stairway and watched the specter walk right through them on several occasions. Following Myers' instructions, Rosina determined that she was unable to either touch the ghost or communicate with her. She also confirmed that the figure appeared solid because she blocked the light, and seemed somewhat aware of her surroundings because she moved around furnishings. The one time she appeared to be aware of Rosina, the spirit gasped in shock and moved quickly away—acting quite as if she had been the one to see a ghost.

Rosina and her father also researched the history of the house and determined that they were being haunted by the spirit of a former occupant, a Mrs. Imogen Swinhoe. The identification raised more questions than it answered, however. Mrs. Swinhoe had been an alcoholic who frequently quarreled with her husband. She had left both Mr. Swinhoe and the house in Cheltenham long before her death—making it rather curious that she would haunt that particular house in the persona of a grieving widow. Still, it was this very realistic lack of storybook tidiness that made the details of the Cheltenham haunting so irresistible to Frederic Myers.

Myers conducted exhaustive interviews with everyone who had ever seen the mysterious woman in black. All in all, he was highly impressed by the consistency of the accounts, the seemingly effortless corroboration of detail. He wrote, "In this case it is observable that the phenomena as seen or heard by all the witnesses were very uniform in character—even in the numerous instances where there had been no previous communication between the percipients." In particular, he found the Despards to be excellent witnesses; they were intelligent and dispassionate, with no desire for public attention. They were quite the opposite, and Myers soon realized that he would have to coax the family to publicize their case. At the time of the investigation, Rosina was a medical student—no small achievement for a woman in Victorian times—and she was likely unwilling to risk her reputation and her career for the sake of psychical research. Her father was equally reluctant about going public with the story; the house on Pittville Circus Road was owned by a friend, and he was concerned that a ghost might decrease its value. In the end, the family consented to let the SPR publish Rosina's detailed account of the case only if it was written under a pseudonym. Thus, in 1892, in volume eight of the journal *Proceedings of the Society for Psychical Research,* a paper entitled "Record of a Haunted House" was written by a Miss R.C. Morton. Though the real names of the people involved were revealed in 1948, this famous case—perhaps the best-documented haunting on record—is often still referred to as "the Morton case."

One particularly interesting fact in this story is that in the early years, the ghost appeared so solid and real that she was often mistaken for a living person. As time passed, she began to look less and less substantial, as though she was losing strength. Fortunately for students of the paranormal, she was seen by at least 17 people before she faded from sight altogether. It would have been a great shame, after all, if no one ever encountered Cheltenham's fascinating lady in black.

# 2
# The
# Spiritualists

*~*

*A darkened room.
A mysterious rapping.
Suddenly, a table lurches
as if moved by unseen
hands. Countless
Victorians abandoned
conventional religion and
embraced spiritualism—
the belief that the dead
walked among them...*

*~*

# Emanuel Swedenborg

It was a pleasant afternoon in July 1759. In the town of Gotenborg, Sweden, a group of 15 people was gathered for a dinner party. One of the guests, the famous scientist Emanuel Swedenborg, had returned to Sweden from England only a few hours earlier. He had not yet been to his home in Stockholm, and in fact had not been there for some time. But as he stepped outside for a breath of fresh air, he suddenly envisioned his familiar home—which was 280 miles away—very clearly.

When Swedenborg rejoined the other guests, they could see that he was highly agitated.

"It is terrible!" he said, wringing his hands in despair. "There is a horrendous fire raging in Stockholm, and it is spreading in the direction of my house!"

The party guests looked at one another nervously. It seemed impossible in 1759 that anyone could know of a fire that was burning nearly 300 miles away. Yet Swedenborg, besides being a renowned man of science, had built a considerable reputation as a seer. Even those at the gathering who were skeptical of such things found themselves paying close attention to his reports of the fire. People who owned homes in Stockholm themselves were particularly attentive.

Swedenborg first "saw" the fire at 6 PM. At 7:30, he announced that it was being brought under control. Then, at 8 PM, he paused suddenly in the middle of a conversation, and joyfully exclaimed, "Thank God! The fire is extinguished the third door from my house!"

It was several days before messengers from Stockholm arrived in Gotenborg. When they did, they brought news of the fire—the report matched, in minute detail, everything Emanuel Swedenborg had said.

It is interesting to note that one of the people who most influenced thinking in the Victorian era did not actually live in Victorian times. Emanuel Swedenborg was a citizen of the 18th century, but his writings and philosophies were destined to inspire the spiritualist movement that would take hold more than 75 years after his death. By then, he was famous primarily for being a tremendously gifted mystic. In his own lifetime, however, he was seen in a different light.

It has often been said that Swedenborg lived his remarkable life in two parts. Until his middle years, he was an outstanding scientist and scholar. He excelled in geology, chemistry, mathematics, metallurgy, astronomy, anatomy and economics. He was multilingual and well traveled. By 1716, King Charles XII of Sweden had named him special assessor to the Royal College of Mines. He published several volumes of scientific works and invented a number of revolutionary devices. Then, in 1743, at the age of 56, Emanuel Swedenborg chose to bring his illustrious career to an abrupt end—all because of a dream.

In Swedenborg's mind, it was more than a dream; he considered it an ecstatic vision. In it, he traveled to both heaven and hell, spoke with God and Jesus, visited with angels and was shown the order and nature of the universe. When he awoke, Swedenborg believed himself to be a messenger, specially chosen to deliver this information to others. He retired from his job on a half-pension so that he was free to devote all his time to spiritual exploration. Many of his colleagues believed that the renowned Swedish genius had lost his mind.

Swedenborg's behavior certainly appeared to be eccentric. He became a semi-recluse who sustained himself primarily with coffee, bread and milk. He learned to induce trances at will, by controlling his breathing, and would sometimes remain in an unconscious state for days at a time. At his own expense, he began to publish books detailing exactly what he saw during those self-induced trances.

In his writings, Emanuel Swedenborg described a spiritual world consisting of three principal realms: Heaven, Hell and the World of Spirits. The last realm acts as a clearing-house of sorts for the newly deceased. Existence in the afterlife is similar to existence on earth, he said; there is work, leisure, government, marriage and even war. Souls are able to advance, but they cannot move from Hell to Heaven, or vice-versa. Time and space both exist, but not as we know them. Furthermore, Swedenborg described Heaven as being boundless, a place that could never become overpopulated. This point was important, considering that, in some of his trances, he had traveled to other planets and found them to be populated with humanoids who were all subject to the same "Divine Law."

Swedenborg's ideas were not at all well received. His fellow intellectuals mocked him and religious authorities spoke out against him. His books were strictly banned by the Swedish government. But Swedenborg could not be discouraged. He continued to communicate with the "angels" and continued to publish his discoveries and observations in a seemingly endless stream of books.

What could not be denied, even by Swedenborg's harshest critics, was that he had developed amazing clairvoyance. The philosopher Immanuel Kant conducted an extensive investigation into Swedenborg's remote viewing of the Stockholm fire, and then he published a summary of his findings. His conclusion was that the incident placed "Swedenborg's extraordinary gifts beyond all possibility of doubt." Queen Louisa Ulrica was similarly impressed by a very personal message that Swedenborg delivered to her from her dead brother, Augustus William. There was a story of a widow who went to the mystic for help when a merchant was demanding payment for a silver service that she was certain her late husband had already paid for. Swedenborg consulted the angels, then told the woman of a secret compartment in her bureau. She went to it and found the receipt for the silver service. Until the last days of his life, Swedenborg astounded people with his sense of intuition and even prophecy. At the age of 84, he wrote a note to a friend in which he predicted the day of his own death one month later.

Still, even those who were impressed by Swedenborg's apparent psychic talents had difficulty in accepting his theories regarding the afterlife. Some people believed that he had indeed been granted a rare vision—but had then misinterpreted much of what he had seen. Even in the 19th century, spiritualists who regarded Swedenborg as a herald chose to ignore many of his claims. Two of his concepts, however, they wholeheartedly embraced: that of survival of the soul, and that of the existence of spirit realms. These ideas alone caused Swedenborg to be regarded as "the father of modern spiritualism."

Few Victorians ever read Emanuel Swedenborg's dry, scholarly books—even after they were translated from Latin into English. So how were they introduced to his philosophies? Through a simple man known as the "Poughkeepsie Seer," Andrew Jackson Davis...

# Andrew Jackson Davis

Andrew Jackson Davis, known through most of his life as the "Poughkeepsie Seer," was born in 1826 to a poor family in Orange County, New York. Davis' mother was deeply religious but illiterate. His abusive father worked on and off as a cobbler and drank heavily. The young Davis was a frail, anxious child who claimed occasionally to hear disembodied voices. The family moved often, so the boy's education was spotty and superficial at best.

In 1843, Davis' world began to change for the better. A Poughkeepsie tailor named William Levingston, who was interested in mesmerism, managed to hypnotize the teenaged Davis. Davis discovered that when he was entranced he could see through the exterior of the human body. He was able to see all of the vital organs, each of which radiated light according to its state of health. Based on what he saw when he was hypnotized, Davis was able to make startlingly accurate medical

*Andrew Jackson Davis, a.k.a. the "Poughkeepsie Seer" and spiritualism's John the Baptist*

diagnoses. He immediately went to work as a clairvoyant and healer. It was then that he became known as the Poughkeepsie Seer.

Davis had been working for a healer for only a few months when he had an experience that changed the course of his life. In March 1844, he entered a trance in which he either wandered or levitated 40 miles from his home to the Catskill Mountains. There, he was visited by the spirits of the Greek physician Galen and the Swedish mystic Emanuel Swedenborg. The two distinguished spirits offered Davis great illumination and wisdom. During this and subsequent visions, Andrew Jackson Davis became convinced that he was meant to serve as an oracle for some divine truth. His true life's work had just begun.

By 1845, Davis was regularly entering trances during which he dictated the rambling text of what would be his first book. After 157 hypnotic sessions, his masterpiece was published. It ran to 782 pages and was entitled *The Principles of Nature, Her Divine Revelations and a Voice to Mankind, By and Through Andrew Jackson Davis, the "Poughkeepsie Seer" and "Clairvoyant."* Although the book was amazingly Swedenborgian in concept, the 21-year-old Davis was poorly educated and had never read the Swedish visionary's works. The controversial book with the ponderous title made Davis an instant celebrity and eventually went into 34 editions.

Andrew Jackson Davis enjoyed a long career as a lecturer, writer and healer. At the age of 60, he earned a medical degree and became a proponent of herbal cures. Despite all that he accomplished, however, he would be remembered primarily as spiritualism's "John the Baptist"—the prophet who foretold the coming of the spiritualist era. Davis had often claimed that the living could communicate with spirits "in higher spheres" and that life after death would one day be proven. The *exact* day was noted in Davis' diary, in an entry dated March 31, 1848. He wrote:

> About daylight this morning a warm breathing passed over my face and I heard a voice, tender and strong, saying: "Brother, the good work has begun—behold a living demonstration is born." I was left wondering what could be meant by such a message.

On the very day that Andrew Jackson Davis was given his message, another message—later interpreted to be Davis' "living demonstration"—was being delivered. In a small farmhouse in Hydesville, New York, a spirit had begun rapping in order to communicate with two young sisters. Their names, soon to be known around the world, were Kate and Maggie Fox...

# The Fox Sisters

On March 31, 1848, an 11-year-old girl named Kate Fox performed a demonstration of sorts for her parents. As Mr. and Mrs. Fox looked on, Kate stood in the middle of her bedroom and spoke in a clear manner.

"Mr. Splitfoot," she said, "do as I do."

The girl clapped her hands exactly three times. Her parents were astounded to hear a reply—three distinct raps—come out of thin air. For some time, the family had been plagued by disturbances that it had attributed to a ghost. Now here was young Kate, claiming that she could communicate with that spirit.

"See, I can do it, too," spoke Maggie, Kate's 14-year-old sister. She clapped her hands five times in a particular rhythm. There was a moment's silence, then the spirit—whom the girls had taken to addressing as "Mr. Splitfoot"—answered in like.

"Do you think...Do you think we could speak to it as well?" asked Mrs. Fox. An answering thud came seemingly out of nowhere. The woman jumped a little, and her hand fluttered nervously to her face.

Mr. Fox cleared his throat.

"Might be a better way to do this," he said. "A way to speak with it, as it were."

There was a way. By the end of the evening, the family had worked out a communication code. The spirit would rap once for "yes," twice for "no" and in response to the letters of the alphabet. It was a tedious process, but it allowed the spirit to "talk."

The ghost claimed to have been a pedlar named Charles Rosa, who had been murdered by previous tenants in the house. His remains were buried beneath the cellar floorboards, he said.

Mr. Fox took a shovel into the cellar the next day. It wasn't long before he found a few scattered bones, some teeth and what appeared to be human hair. It was proof enough for the family, which began to share the sensational story with others. Before long, many of the Foxes' neighbors were dropping by to witness the phenomenon for themselves. "Mr. Splitfoot," a.k.a. "Charles Rosa," never disappointed the guests. Soon, everyone in Hydesville was talking about the little Fox sisters and their noisy spirit friend.

The story might have ended there, had it not been for Kate's and Maggie's enterprising older sister, Leah Fox Fish. Leah, in her mid-30s, had been looking for a way to support herself and her daughter ever since being deserted by her husband. She was by all accounts a shrewd woman who recognized a great opportunity in Kate and Maggie and their rapping ghost. Leah wasted no time in making her way to Hydesville. Once there, she took charge of her younger sisters and what she hoped would be their marketable new talent.

Leah Fish turned the girls into a profitable, popular stage act. Everywhere they appeared, rapping spirits also appeared, prepared to amaze audiences. After a short time, as the girls' "mediumship abilities" blossomed, the séances grew more spectacular, with levitating objects and visits from such eminent spirits as Benjamin Franklin. Skeptics inevitably tried to expose Kate and Maggie as

*Maggie Fox, who denounced spiritualism and confessed to being a fraudulent medium in 1888*

frauds, but none were successful. Their popularity continued to grow, and thousands of people who had been dab-
bling in mesmerism and Swedenborgianism considered
them to be the long-awaited proof of life after death. And,
religious and philosophical considerations aside, the Fox

sisters were a serious money-making proposition. Leah Fish was finally earning a good living, taking her cut even from the likes of P.T. Barnum, who once brought the girls to perform in New York City.

But despite their success, all was not well with Kate and Maggie. By 1855, both were exhausted from years of touring and had begun to drink heavily. By 1857, Leah had tired of managing her sisters' careers and had found a wealthy businessman to marry. She left the girls on their own. Soon after, Maggie Fox announced that she had grown disillusioned with the spiritualist movement and was converting to Catholicism. Kate continued to perform alone, expanding her act to include feats such as mirror writing (reverse automatic writing, which had to be held to a mirror to be read) and the visual manifestation of spirits. Her alcoholism continued to escalate, however, and she was considered to be unreliable.

It was more than three decades before Kate and Maggie Fox appeared together on stage again. When they did, in 1888, it was to denounce spiritualism and confess to their own fraud. They claimed that, since the beginning, they had created the rapping sounds by cracking the joints in their toes. They said that Leah had encouraged them to take their trickery public because she sensed that the time was right to create a new religion.

Leah never responded to the accusations. Dedicated spiritualists refused to believe the confession. Kate and Maggie went on a tour to expose spiritualism, but it did not last long. Even before the tour had ended, Kate had returned to working as a medium. By 1891, Maggie had publicly recanted her confession.

In the end, neither of the two sisters had lived a particularly long or happy life. Kate died in 1892 at the age of 56, of acute alcoholism. By the following year, 59-year-old Maggie was destitute and dying at a friend's house in Brooklyn. According to one issue of *Strange Magazine*, the doctor who was commissioned to care for her might have been the only one, in the end, to know whether Maggie truly had mediumistic abilities. According to that report, just before she slipped into a coma, Maggie Fox (then going by the name Margaretta Kane) asked her doctor for a pen and paper. Once she had them, she wrote at a feverish pace that belied her weakened condition.

"Here," she said to the doctor, when she had finished. "These are for you."

Maggie gave her doctor some 20 pages covered in neat script. The doctor read them and was amazed to find that she was reading the story of her own life, including personal details that she had never shared with another living being. What was most startling, however, was information about a will that had been secreted away by the doctor's mother before her death. The doctor immediately contacted her brother and gave him the instructions that had been given to her by Maggie Fox. Within a short time, the missing will was recovered.

This obscure story aside, it remains to be proven whether Kate and Maggie Fox were gifted mediums, able to converse with spirits, or opportunistic tricksters and frauds. Either way, their actions ensured their place in history. However one might regard them, it is a fact that they were instrumental in the birth of modern spiritualism.

# Séances in High Places

In the book *Mysteries of the Unknown: Spirit Summonings* (Time-Life Books, 1989), it is noted that "spiritualism listed in its ranks some of the finest minds of its day. Philosophical, political and literary luminaries were among its converts, and renowned scientists gave it serious study." It is true that the concept appealed to people in all walks of life, including those in positions of great influence. As a result, mediums and their spirit controls had access to some of the most important and powerful people of the day. There is little doubt that, to some degree, spiritualism managed to alter the course of social history.

The author Harriet Beecher Stowe was a spiritualist, and it has often been suggested that spirits guided the writing of her influential book, *Uncle Tom's Cabin*. Czar Alexander II consulted mediums, and many spiritualists believe that it was otherworldly advice that led him to free the Russian serfs. Similarly, in the White House, Abraham Lincoln was said to be influenced by spirits to issue the Emancipation Proclamation.

It is a matter of historical fact that Lincoln was intrigued by spiritualism and fascinated by the phenomena produced at séances. Countless séances were held in the White House during his presidency, many of which were well documented and even made public at the time. On April 12, 1863, the *Chicago Tribune* ran an article detailing a spiritual gathering held in the Crimson Room. A medium named Charles E. Shockle presided over the affair. For a period of some 30 minutes, it was reported that tables moved, rapping was heard, two candelabra were raised to the ceiling and a portrait of Henry Clay was seen to sway more than a foot. During another well-publicized event, a physical medium by the name of Mrs. Miller twice lifted a grand piano into the air by simply placing her hand upon it. During the second display, the president and two other astonished men were sitting on top of the instrument as it levitated.

Other mediums known to perform in the White House included J.B Conklin, Mrs. Cranston Laurie and Miss Nettie Coburn. Coburn, it is said, was frequently consulted by Lincoln during the worst crises of the Civil War. According to Susy Smith in *Prominent American Ghosts* (Dell, 1967):

> Through her mouth when she was in a trance great leaders in the spirit world purported to speak, and the advice they gave was so wise that Lincoln took it under very careful advisement. He is reported to have told Miss Coburn, "My child, you possess a most singular gift; that it is of God, I have no doubt."

Eventually, Nettie Coburn claimed to have been instrumental in bringing forth the Emancipation Proclamation, saying that her spirit controls advised Lincoln that only by freeing the slaves would he bring about an end to the war.

Cora Richmond, a friend of Coburn's who rose to great fame as a medium, was similarly eager to take credit for significant government decisions. She asserted that

Lincoln and the Joint Congressional Committee on Reconstruction had actively sought her advice. Though Richmond did have ties to the White House, this particular claim of hers has always been dismissed by historians.

The same skeptics could not deny that Queen Victoria was a spiritualist who regularly sought the advice of her dead husband through mediums. Even during her lifetime, it was widely known and accepted that John Brown, the churlish Scottish servant appointed to be in "constant personal attendance upon Her Majesty on all occasions," acted as that link to the next world. From the June 20, 1883, edition of the *Toronto World:*

> That the queen is not only "a mild believer in Spiritualism," but is in full possession of the facts of the philosophy, there can be no doubt, and, incredible as it may appear to those who have not given the subject any thought, she did actually receive assistance from the late prince consort "in working out questions which perplexed and annoyed her." What was the cause of the great attachment of the queen to her late personal attendant, John Brown, has been a wonder to many, yet it is not at all surprising when it is known that he was the medium through whom she held these interviews with her husband.

Certainly, Queen Victoria's relationship with Brown was unusually close. She described herself as "his truest, best and most faithful friend." The queen lived up to that description after Brown's death, memorializing him with a touching inscription on his tombstone. It reads:

That friend on whose fidelity you count, that friend given you by circumstances over which you have no control, was God's own gift.

The inscription stands as everlasting proof of one medium's influence over the most powerful ruler of the 19th century.

# Worth a Thousand Words: The Era of Spirit Photography

In 1861, a Boston photographer by the name of William Mumler developed a self-portrait that revealed a shadowy image of his deceased cousin. He showed it to a medium who announced that it was, in fact, a "spirit portrait" and that Mumler's cousin had chosen photography as a way to communicate with the living. Mumler found that there were seemingly countless spirits anxious to communicate through his pictures. He began offering his services to those who wished to have one last portrait taken with their dearly departed, and the business of spirit photography was born.

Eight years later, according to the New York *Sun*, Mumler's business was booming. In one paragraph of a lengthy article regarding his success, the writer explained what Mumler's portraits were like:

Mr. Mumler has preserved 100 or so of the more remarkable photographs taken, and our reporter saw and examined them. They all present likenesses of living persons, which look exactly as ordinary photographs do, being, indeed, taken in the regular way. But behind, or at one side of the living sitter, appears sometimes only a head, sometimes a head and shoulders, and sometimes the full length of another person, rather indistinct and shadowy, but still in many cases clearly enough defined for a likeness to be recognized.

At the end of the article it was noted that "the whole thing is a marvel...and deserves to be investigated by scientific men."

In the end, no rigorous scientific investigation was required. Mumler's work was quite thoroughly debunked by a number of people who noticed that several of the "spirits" in his photos strongly resembled Bostonians who were alive and well. William Mumler was arrested for fraud, but not before the fad of spirit photography had gained incredible momentum.

Believers flocked to the studios of "spirit photographers" to see what phantom figures might turn up alongside them in their portraits. Translucent images of "extras," as the ghostly images were called, would typically appear floating in the air around the subject. Occasionally, a famous face would be among the spirits. Often, there were Native American spirit guides in full headdresses. Of course, the photographers were reluctant to disappoint their clients— so they often relied upon trickery to achieve the desired effect. Photographs were frequently doctored through the use of double exposures and other fraudulent methods.

*A typical example of spirit photography, featuring many ghostly "extras"*

As more and more spectral images were revealed to be outright fakes, the popularity of spirit photography declined. It simply came to a point where few people were willing to believe that phantoms sat to have their portraits taken. That was not to say that no one believed that the image of a ghost could be captured on film. Paranormal researchers continue, to this day, to take photographs as a routine part of their investigations in the hope that some inexplicable shape will show up in the negatives. It is also worth noting that, over the years, there have been countless cases where someone has innocently snapped a picture only to discover upon developing the film that an apparition made its way into the shot. With few exceptions, these photographed phantoms can usually be explained away as the natural effects of light, shadow or random patterns in the background. Paranormal photographs today come under a much more scrupulous eye than did the miraculous images produced in William Mumler's era of spirit photography.

# Lily Dale and Cassadaga: Communities of Spirits

It is estimated that somewhere between 20,000 and 30,000 people visit the tiny spiritualist community of Lily Dale, New York, each year. They stay at the Maplewood Hotel and eat at the Lily Dale Cafeteria and the Pagoda. They gather to hear spirits deliver messages at Forest Temple. They buy trinkets and crystals at the new age stores and participate in workshops and lectures on topics ranging from psychic pet communication to past-life regression. They pay for readings with mediums, all of whom have been certified by the Lily Dale Assembly. And, as they walk along the winding paths that cut through the woods or down streets lined with gingerbread-trimmed, Victorian houses, they may feel that they have stepped back in time.

A visit to the Lily Dale Museum proves that many things are indeed just as they were more than a century ago. Many of the buildings date back to the late 1800s and many of the rituals, such as the meetings at Forest Temple, go on just as they did in the Victorian era. Most significantly, Lily Dale's purpose has not changed in 125 years: it remains a place where spiritualists can discuss their beliefs and practice their healing and mediumship. That is what Lily Dale has been about ever since it was founded.

In the late 19th century, a certain area of New York State became so well known for its "fires" of religious revival that it was eventually nicknamed the "burned-over district." Mormonism was born there; the Shakers established their Holy Sanctuary of the New World there; the Fox sisters first heard a mysterious rapping there (see page 68); and some of the earliest, most dedicated spiritualists gathered there. In 1879, those same spiritualists purchased 20 acres of land from a local farmer for the sum of $1845. This picturesque area became the home of the Lily Dale Assembly.

In its early days, Lily Dale was a magnetic place that drew dynamic speakers, curious celebrities and passionate social reformers. The summers were idyllic, and people sometimes spent the entire season boating, bicycling and hobnobbing with the spirits. The New York winters could be harsh, however, so some of Lily Dale's mediums began making an annual pilgrimage to Florida. At first they camped in tent communities. After a while, a permanent church and an assembly hall were built. A few houses followed. By 1894, the tiny town—named "Cassadaga"—was an official year-round residence for many mediums, offering spiritualists a warm-weather alternative to Lily Dale.

Today, Cassadaga is also a quaint, historic place, caught in time much the way its sister community of Lily Dale appears to be. The streets are narrow, the oak and magnolia trees are overgrown and most of the small frame houses date back to at least the 1920s. Many of those modest houses are marked with old-fashioned, hand-lettered signs declaring that a "Spiritual Counselor" or "Medium" resides within. Most tourists take the time to indulge in a reading, even if their initial plan was to simply enjoy the historic ambiance of the place.

*Mediums deliver messages from spirits at Lily Dale's Forest Temple.*

A few minutes down the highway, the atmosphere is decidedly more modern. Splashy neon signs and big-box stores are beginning to crowd the borders of Cassadaga. For now, the mood of this eccentric little community—and that of its northern sister, Lily Dale—remains peaceful, calm and, yes, decidedly spiritual. Those wishing to peer into the future need only take a step into the past—into one of these two Victorian communities of spirits.

# Rulers of the Darkened Room

Throughout history, people have claimed to gain wisdom from mysterious and unseen forces. They called themselves soothsayers, oracles, wizards, shamans, medicine men, sorcerers, mystics, priests and prophets. Their ability to communicate with spirits was understood to be a rare gift, a gift of divine origin that could not be easily acquired. All that changed in 1848 when the Fox sisters began communicating with the ghost that haunted their shabby little farmhouse in New York State. People were inspired by the girls' ordinariness. If two schoolgirls of average intelligence could speak with the dead, one had to wonder if perhaps anybody could. Within a few years, that appeared to be the case. Spiritualism spread like an epidemic, and mediums could be found everywhere. It was estimated that by the mid-1850s, there were as many as 30,000 mediums working in the United States alone.

In darkened parlors across Europe and North America, tables danced, tambourines shook and spirits rapped out miraculous messages. Some mediums channeled the dead, falling into dramatic trances that allowed the spirits to speak through them. Some phantoms preferred to write their communications on slates or to play instruments with invisible hands. Others would materialize in a ghostly, glowing form and walk among the amazed sitters. When conducted by a professional medium, a séance could be truly spectacular.

The pros were highly sought after. Although spiritualists believed that anyone could talk to the dead, professional mediums were much more proficient at getting the dead to talk back. That may have been because they were extraordinarily gifted—or it may have been that they knew all the tricks of the trade. Communicating with the spirit world was a booming business, and as with all businesses, there were frauds. Mediums were frequently masters of stagecraft who exploited their clients' vulnerability and credulity. Standard deceptions were often as simple as "levitating" a table by lifting it with one's foot, or surreptitiously exchanging a blank slate for one with "spirit writing" that had been prepared beforehand. Mediums were adept at planting a suggestion in the mind of the sitter and then confirming it with false evidence. For example, a medium who was supposedly secured in a cabinet would announce that she was levitating, while an assistant in the darkened room would lightly brush a pair of shoes across the top of the sitter's head. By the end of the 19th century, such cons were so common that a Chicago mail order company put out a catalogue of trick devices, ranging from luminous masks to spring-loaded slates, guaranteed to create phenomenal séance effects. Many of the most effective ploys were deceptively simple—for example, mediums would often stop in mid-séance and announce that the "spirits" had demanded that some people in the circle leave the room. The banished were almost always those whom the medium knew to be skeptical and, therefore, a risk to have in attendance. Believers were much easier to dupe, because they *expected* to be amazed.

For the genuine and fraudulent alike, the profession of mediumship opened new doors. Women, in particular, enjoyed an unexpected reprieve from the constraints of Victorian life. In an era when females had few rights and were considered to be inferior to men in every way, channeling provided them with an unprecedented opportunity to publicly voice their opinions and even earn a modest income for doing so. Women and men flocked to see "trance lecturers" who would pontificate for hours on a variety of subjects. The audiences paid close attention because the spirits who spoke through the mediums were intelligent, well spoken and, therefore, obviously male. It was an assumption that granted female mediums a large degree of power and influence—not to mention the freedom to behave as she wished. People would tolerate coarse, unladylike behavior from a female medium who was on stage or conducting a séance, believing that masculine spirits were forcing her into it.

One medium who made great use of this advantage was Emma Hardinge Britten. Britten was an English medium and well-known trance lecturer who was said to be gifted in the areas of automatic writing, healing, psychometry and prophecy. Though she founded the spiritual newspaper *Two Worlds* and organized the Spiritualists' National Union in Britain, she may be best known for her contribution of "The Principles of Spiritualism," six laws by which all believers were required to abide. Victorians might have had difficulty accepting such crucial direction from a woman, so Britten ensured that they wouldn't have to. She simply claimed that it was actually Robert Owen, the acclaimed socialist reformer, who authored the principles after his death and then channeled them through her.

An American medium by the name of Cora Richmond found similar success through similar methods. She, too, was a trance lecturer who could speak for hours at a time on subjects that were traditionally the domain of men. Her most famous speech of all time, entitled "A Message to the Nation," was supposedly delivered through her by none other than the spirit of the assassinated U.S. president, James A. Garfield.

Another woman of that time—not a medium, but a devoted spiritualist—would never have been satisfied by merely channeling a president. Victoria Woodhull wanted to *be* president, and she made history in 1872 by being the first woman to ever take a run at the Oval Office. Her views on religion, feminism and sexual freedom ensured that she was not only defeated at the polls but was financially and emotionally battered in the process. Woodhull eventually moved to England, married a respected banker and gave up public life altogether.

Woodhull was never alone in her beliefs. Many spiritualists and mediums were social reformers at heart, calling upon distinguished and famous spirits to give voice to their own personal views on abolition, women's suffrage and free love. Others were champions only for themselves. Of the mediums in this group, none was more colorful than "the Medium of Kings and King of Mediums," Daniel Dunglas Home.

*An artist's conception of D.D. Home demonstrating his ability to levitate*

Home (pronounced "Hume") was born in 1833 in a small town in Scotland, but he was raised primarily in

Connecticut. He demonstrated mediumistic abilities as early as infancy; his aunt reported that his cradle was able to rock itself. By 1855, Home had grown into an ambitious young man, and he decided that he would move to England to try his hand at conjuring spirits for the rich and royal. Understanding the importance of social class in Europe, Home went to the trouble of reinventing himself before he set sail. He added to his name "Dunglas," a common moniker among the Scottish earls of Home, and fabricated a vague story of an aristocratic family history. The deceit served him well. Using this genteel persona, along with his good looks, effusive charm and considerable talents as a medium, Home gained access to the best social circles with enviable ease. He conducted séances for Czar Alexander II of Russia, Napoleon III of France and an assortment of kings and queens around Continental Europe. He managed to impress various literary greats, including William Makepeace Thackeray, Ivan Turgenev and Alexandre Dumas, *père*. In all cases, Home would accept no money for his services. In all likelihood, it was calculated generosity that paid off handsomely. Though he was never wealthy in his own right, Home lived the lifestyle of a rich man, owing to the hospitality of his generous patrons. His presence was much sought after; he became the consummate houseguest, supported by his admirers in a truly grand fashion.

In a sense, Home did earn his keep. He was a witty conversationalist, a competent pianist and a generally entertaining fellow. It was when he called upon the spirits, however, that his true talents showed. He was able to shorten or elongate his body by nearly a foot, and he could produce ghostly lights and glowing, disembodied hands. The spirits often played music at Home's séances and rapped out messages. It was also reported that the medium could handle red-hot coals without injury. Perhaps most impressive was Home's ability to levitate furniture, objects and even himself. His most famous feat took place in 1868, in the London home of Lord Adare. In front of several credible witnesses, an entranced Home floated out of a third-floor window, drifted alongside the house and then reentered through a different window. According to the Earl of Crawford, who was present at the time, "The distance between the windows was about seven feet six inches, and there was not the slightest foothold between them..."

Home was the subject of investigations, as well as a participant in an extensive series of tests with the eminent scientist Sir William Crookes. Crookes concluded that Home possessed an independent psychic force. As for others who attempted to debunk the medium, none was ever successful in doing so. D.D. Home was never caught in an act of fraud—but that is not to say that he escaped scandal. In 1867 he was sued by a wealthy widow who claimed that he had swindled her out of 60,000 pounds. The resulting trial was an embarrassment to all who were involved. The court eventually found in the widow's favor, but not before speaking out harshly against the plaintiff, the defendant and spiritualism in general. Another severe blow to Home's reputation came with the poet Robert Browning's publication of "Mr. Sludge, 'the Medium',￼" a scathing work that was obviously about Home (see page 114). The medium suffered some loss of popularity on

*A notice advertising a performance by the amazing Davenport Brothers*

both occasions, but managed to recover. His sheer ability always saw him through. Whether that was an ability to conjure spirits or an ability to manipulate impressionable people was never determined to any satisfying degree.

As a man, Home was somewhat rare among mediums. It was generally accepted that women, being weak minded and easily influenced, were more likely to be good spirit channels. Still, Home was not alone. William Stainton Moses was said to be a powerful physical medium of Home's ilk, and journalist William Stead, while not prescient enough to avoid boarding the *Titanic,* was an energetic champion of spiritualism who was said to be gifted with second sight. But for pure spectacle and entertainment, no men outdid the dazzling Davenport Brothers.

William and Ira Davenport never claimed to be mediums, but spiritualists of the day were eager to point out that the brothers could not possibly have done what they did without the aid of invisible hands. Every Davenport show was a fantastic display of music and special visual effects, all of which were produced as the brothers sat securely tied within an enclosed cabinet. In their time, the Davenports were widely believed to have genuine mediumistic powers. After the turn of the 20th century, however, most people were of the opinion that the brothers were brilliant illusionists.

Of course, all mediums were performers to some extent, even if they never stepped on a stage. A flair for drama and great personal magnetism were valuable assets in the spirit business—and no one was more endowed with those qualities than Madame Helena Petrovna Blavatsky.

Madame Blavatsky, when described, always sounded unappealing. By all accounts, she was overweight, sloppily dressed and mean tempered. She was a chain smoker and a known drug user. But those who met her and gazed into her hypnotic, azure eyes were helpless to resist the power of her personality. It was this quality that enabled the Russian immigrant to become a successful medium in New York and to found "Theosophy," her own mystical religion that at her death boasted at least 100,000 followers. Those who were not under her spell tended to be more critical of her mediumistic skills. In 1884, the Society for Psychical Research investigated Blavatsky and concluded, "we regard her...as one of the most accomplished, ingenious and interesting impostors in history."

Many other investigations of mediums produced results that were not nearly so cut and dried. The Italian medium Eusapia Palladino was a famously unpleasant woman and a notorious cheat—but when she was restrained by investigators, she managed to produce amazing, genuine phenomena. The scientists were stumped. If Palladino was a true medium, why did she resort to trickery? The eventual conclusion was that she frequently indulged in fraud to please or impress clients who had come to her on a "low-energy" day. This habitual method of compensation forced psychic investigators to consider something that they had not thought of in previous cases: when a medium was caught cheating *one* time, it didn't conclusively prove that she cheated *all* of the time.

One medium who likely did cheat all of the time was Florence Cook, though the one investigator who should

*A likeness of Madame Helena Petrovna Blavatsky, with the symbol of the Theosophical Society shown above her head*

have easily unmasked her seemed either unwilling or unable to catch her in an act of fraud. Sir William

*Eusapia Palladino, a talented Italian medium who nevertheless frequently resorted to trickery*

Crookes, the noted British physicist, chemist and inventor who had rigorously tested D.D. Home, proved woefully inadequate during his five-month investigation of the medium. Cook was famous for the full-figure materializations of her beautiful "spirit control" Katie King. During séances, while Cook was tied up behind a curtain, an exceedingly pale, white-robed Katie would walk among the sitters, smiling and nodding. After the spirit left, the guests would wait for a certain amount of time, as per Cook's instructions, then draw back the curtain. Cook would be as they had left her, with her hands and feet bound, but exhausted from the channeling experience. When more and more people began to complain that Katie King looked suspiciously like Florence Cook, Crookes began his investigation. But his methods were lax, and he ultimately appeared more concerned with documenting the differences, rather than the similarities, that he noted between the medium and the spirit. In one instance, Cook lay down on a sofa behind a curtain and draped a shawl around her head. A few minutes later, the pallid Katie King appeared from behind the same curtain. While the "spirit" stood in full view, Crookes checked the sofa. A female form, which he assumed to be Cook's, still lay there. It seems unbelievable that, without lifting the shawl to verify the woman's identity, Crookes declared that he had just seen Florence Cook and Katie King together in the same room, thereby proving that they were not the same person. It was suggested by many that Crookes' judgment was clouded because he was either infatuated or romantically involved with the lovely medium, or that he dared not expose her, for fear that she would reveal their affair and destroy his reputation. In the end, it didn't matter—several other people caught Cook in outrageous and obvious acts of fraud and her career rapidly declined. Florence Cook was disgraced and impoverished when she died in 1904.

Even without the interference of investigators, Florence Cook would have had her troubles. Her petite beauty won her many admirers, but it inspired an envious hatred in a rival medium, Agnes Guppy. When Guppy was not busy spewing poisonous comments about Cook, she was often producing her famous "apports," objects that materialized out of nowhere. At the séance sitter's request, Guppy's spirits would drop any number of things from the ceiling; over the years they produced sunflowers, starfish, cacti, lobsters and other wonders. But the grossly overweight Guppy was most famous for having once apported herself two miles away from her home. She was working on her household accounts with a friend when she suddenly vanished—only to appear, in her dressing gown with her accounts book in her hand, in the middle of a table where two of her proteges were conducting a séance.

Agnes Guppy's abilities were well documented, but her vile personality was her undoing. A Nobel Prize–winning physicist once wrote, "Mrs. Guppy I don't think I could stand, even in the cause of science." When it was eventually discovered that Guppy had once conspired to have acid thrown in Florence Cook's "doll face," the spiritualist community was horrified. At that point, Agnes Guppy lost what few supporters she had left and her career ground to a halt.

Toward the end of the 19th century, there was a woman from Boston who became the forerunner of a completely

*Medium Florence Cook, appearing as her "spirit control," Katie King*

different breed of mediums. Her name was Leonora Piper, and there were no theatrics in her séances. The table remained on the floor, no instruments played and the spirits could be depended upon to *not* materialize. But despite this lack of action, Piper was truly extraordinary. She impressed everyone whom she read for, including the preeminent American psychologist William James. James was the brother of novelist Henry James and a renowned Harvard psychologist and philosopher. He may have been the most influential and respected thinker to ever venture into the area of psychic research and for many years, the subject of his investigation was Piper. When she was in a trance, she knew things about James and his family that he himself did not even know at the time. Her consistent, impressive performances led him to write, "Taking everything I know of Mrs. P. into account, the result is to make me feel as absolutely certain as I am of any personal fact in the world that she knows things in her trances which she cannot possibly have heard in her waking state." At a later date, he concluded, "If you wish to upset the law that all crows are black, you must not seek to show that no crows are: it is enough if you prove one single crow to be white." Leonora Piper was William James' one white crow; she proved to him the existence of supernormal powers.

What James never established to his satisfaction was whether Piper's powers were spiritual or psychic. The medium herself never insisted that she was channeling spirits; in fact, she openly wondered whether she actually suffered from some undiagnosed mental condition. But all the researchers to ever test her—and there were many over her lifetime—agreed on one thing: Leonora Piper possessed a truly remarkable gift. They just weren't sure of its exact nature.

It was the beginning of the end for spiritualism. Physical mediums fell out of favor as researchers turned their attention to subjects like telepathy and clairvoyance.

The unexplored powers of the mind, rather than the afterlife, became the focus of investigation. This created a fascinating new field of study, but it steered focus away from spirit communication. The result was that, as Victoria's reign neared its end, the spirits were beginning to grow quiet.

Some people must have wondered if they had ever spoken at all.

# 3
# Haunted Victorian Storytellers

*~*

*Poe...Hawthorne...*
*Dickens...Maupassant...*
*Many of the most popular*
*Victorian authors chose to*
*write about a dark world*
*of spirits and mystery.*
*Perhaps it was because*
*they—and many of their*
*contemporaries—had*
*experienced the*
*supernatural in their*
*own lives...*

*~*

# Edgar Allan Poe

Sir Arthur Conan Doyle called him "the supreme original short-story writer of all time." More than 150 years after his death, he is still considered to be a master craftsman of mystery, suspense and gothic horror, and his tales remain the standard by which all other dark fiction is judged. If there was one author of the Victorian era whose name was synonymous with terror, it was Edgar Allan Poe.

Although Poe certainly was gifted with a vivid imagination, he drew on real-life events more than many of his readers have ever been aware. "The Cask of Amontillado" was based upon a secret murder that Poe learned about when he was a young soldier stationed at Fort Independence on Castle Island. "The Masque of the Red Death" is believed to reflect the author's haunting fear of tuberculosis—a disease that ravaged and claimed many of his loved ones, most notably his mother, Elizabeth, and his young wife, Virginia. And then, most remarkably, there is the true tale that mirrors Poe's famous novella, *The Narrative of Arthur Gordon Pym of Nantucket*.

Poe's story involves three shipwrecked sailors who resort to murdering and cannibalizing a lowly cabin boy to survive their ordeal at sea. As dramatic as the plot seems, the grim details were nearly identical to those brought forth in one of the most famous British court cases of the 19th century. It was the trial of three men—Thomas Dudley, Edwin Stephens and Edmund Brooks—who stood accused of murdering their cabin boy to keep themselves alive after being shipwrecked in a hurricane.

*Edgar Allan Poe—the unchallenged master of the horror story*

Dudley was a ship's captain who was commissioned by a wealthy Australian to sail his newly purchased 50-foot yacht, the *Mignonette,* from Southampton to Sydney. Dudley hired a crew of three men and set sail on May 19. All went well until July 3, when—hundreds of miles from land in the South Atlantic—the *Mignonette* encountered the fury of a hurricane. Gale-force winds and crashing waves sank the vessel, forcing the four men aboard to take refuge in a single, fragile dinghy. In the panic to save their lives, Captain

Dudley and his crew had no time to salvage either drinking water or provisions. As the yacht vanished into the churning ocean, the men realized that they had been left with nothing but their lives and a single tin of parsnips.

Nearly three nightmarish weeks ensued. In that span of time, the starving sailors managed to capture a sea turtle, which they tore apart with their hands and devoured. There had been a day of rain, and the rainwater that they caught served to stave off critical dehydration. Still, after 19 days adrift at sea, the situation was desperate, and the unthinkable notion of cannibalism was sounding ever more reasonable. It was eventually decided that the four men would draw lots to decide which of them would be sacrificed so that the others might live. It sounded fair, but it was not—Dudley, Stephens and Brooks had already decided that their low-ranking cabin boy, who was clearly close to death, should be the one to go. The doomed 17-year-old was murdered by the other three men in the dinghy. His body provided them with sustenance enough that they survived until they were finally rescued by a German sailing barque, the *Montezuma*—a vessel named after the cannibal king of the Aztecs.

The three survivors freely shared their harrowing tale of survival—including the unpleasant details surrounding the cabin boy's death. They felt that they had done nothing wrong, given that the boy would have died anyway and that they needed to sacrifice him to ensure their own survival. But others saw it differently. When the *Montezuma* landed, Dudley, Stephens and Brooks were all arrested. At the end of their famous, sensational trial, all three were found guilty of murder and cannibalism and sentenced to terms of hard labor. The judge—and the general public—had been unwilling to accept as justifiable the grisly killing and feasting described in the courtroom and in Poe's book.

> ...he fell instantly dead. I must not dwell upon the fearful repast which immediately ensued. Such things may be imagined, but words have no power to impress the mind with the exquisite horror of their reality. Let it suffice to say that, having in some measure appeased the raging thirst which consumed us by the blood of the victim, and having by common consent taken off the hands, feet and head, throwing them together with the entrails, into the sea, we devoured the rest of the body, piecemeal...

Edgar Allan Poe's treatment of the story, in *The Narrative of Arthur Gordon Pym of Nantucket,* never strayed far from the details of the real-life event. The number of men aboard the vessel, the cruel storm at sea, the eating of the turtle and the drinking of precious rainwater—all can be found in Poe's account. The drawing of lots and the suggestion that the contest was rigged so as not to be fair is included. Even the name of the unlucky cabin boy is the same: Richard Parker. Yet Poe published his story as fiction. The reason why becomes apparent when the dates of Poe's publication and the infamous shipwreck are added for consideration...the *Mignonette* went down in 1884—a full 35 years after Poe's death and nearly 50 years after the publication of his unsavory tale.

It was a case of incredibly eerie coincidence, one fitting for such a true master of horror as Edgar Allan Poe.

# Henry James

The American-turned-British writer Henry James was perhaps most famous for his classic novella, *The Turn of the Screw*. It was written in 1897 and was first published as a 12-part serial in *Colliers Weekly* magazine. What is particularly interesting is that James wrote it, one of the most famous ghost stories of the Victorian era, to finance his move from London to the picturesque town of Rye in East Sussex. And it was there—in the brick-fronted, early-18th century dwelling known as Lamb House—where Henry James would experience his own personal true-to-life ghost story.

Henry James' interest in the supernatural was evident early in his career, beginning with his 1868 story "The Romance of Certain Old Clothes," in which a woman is murdered by the ghost of her husband's first wife. It was an interest that was understandable, given the intellectual climate in which he lived. Not only was society as a whole opening its mind toward the possibility of the paranormal, but James' father was a long-time member of the Society for Psychical Research. James' father devoted much of his life to the study of theology, philosophy and mysticism, and followed the teachings of Emanuel Swedenborg (see page 60). Henry James grew up well versed in the spiritualistic doctrine of the day. Perhaps because of this background, he felt that an important distinction had to be made between ghosts of the literary variety and those of the modern scientific era. He called the latter "poor subjects," as it were, unable to stir "the dear old sacred terror" in the same way that a good old-fashioned ghost story could. It was an interesting observation and one that he was well qualified to make—by the time he wrote the comments for a preface to the 1908 edition of *The Turn of the Screw,* he had been living with his own ghost in Lamb House for a full decade.

During those years and several that followed, James spoke to friends about the paranormal goings-on in Lamb House. He said that he was often bothered by poltergeist activity and that he was frequently visited by the ghost of a little old lady wearing a mantilla, who was of great assistance to him when he was writing. No one else ever saw James' spectral muse until several years after his death.

It was when another author, E.F. Benson, was living in Lamb House that some American tourists asked to have their photo taken outside the famous house. When the film was developed, there was a mysterious image in one of the front windows—it appeared that an elderly woman was gazing out through the glass. The photographer was curious enough to call E.F. Benson. The writer said that there had been no old woman in the house at the time the picture was taken.

Benson and a later tenant of Lamb House, Rumer Godden, eventually lent credence to the other claims that Henry James made regarding the spirits of the house. Both reported poltergeist activity in the historic abode. At the first sign of such otherworldly action, Rumer Godden wasted no time in having Lamb House blessed by a priest. One has to assume that if the blessing cleared the house of the poltergeist, it likely also got rid of the old lady. Because Godden was also a writer, the blessing may have been a mistake made in haste: although the poltergeist was no doubt a nuisance, the woman in the mantilla was said to be a helpful spirit. Henry James did write three books during the years he lived in Lamb House: *The Ambassadors, The Wings of the Dove* and *The Golden Bowl*. Though he penned each of these novels while working alone in the traditional sense, he did offer credit where it was due: James always maintained that he was "helped" by the semi-transparent, mantilla-wearing muse who walked the halls of his historic Rye home.

# Mark Twain

America's beloved author and humorist Mark Twain once said "I don't believe in ghosts, but they scare the hell out of me." It is not known what he thought of other supernatural phenomena, but chances are that he kept an open mind. In fact, according to Rosemary Ellen Guiley's *Encyclopedia of Ghosts and Spirits* (Facts on File, 1992), Twain once had a firsthand experience with what is known as an "arrival case."

Guiley described an arrival case as follows:

> The appearance of a person in advance of his actual arrival. The arriving phantom appears in the same clothing worn by the person at the time. Observers, believing the individual to be physically present, may speak to the phantom, and it may respond. The projecting individual usually is not aware of

appearing in a distant location until he or she is told about it.

The arrival case experience that Mark Twain had took place at a large reception. Twain had been there for a while when he happened to look across the room and see a particular woman whom he knew well and liked. Twain began to make his way through the crowd of people, attempting to cross the room to where he had seen his lady friend. But the groups of party-goers were pressed tightly together, leaving little room to maneuver. Frequently someone would stop Twain with a greeting or a handshake. By the time he had managed to cross the large room, the woman was nowhere to be seen. Twain knew that he would easily be able to find her later because she had been wearing a most distinctive dress.

Later that day, at the dinner following the reception, Mark Twain saw the woman again. He spotted her quickly among the others at the table, because she wore the same dress she had worn earlier in the day. Twain greeted his friend warmly and said that he regretted missing the opportunity to speak with her at the reception. As he listened to her response, his regret changed to astonishment.

"Yes, I was sorry to miss the party," she said, "but I was unable to catch an earlier train. It's lucky that I didn't miss this dinner as well for *I've only just arrived.*"

Mark Twain had seen his friend's identically dressed phantom double—hours in advance of her actual physical presence.

# The Brownings

In a letter dated January 10, 1845, Robert Browning wrote: "I love your verses with all my heart, dear Miss Barrett—I do, as I say, love your verses with all my heart." So began the most famous courtship of the 19th century. In the 20 months following that initial correspondence, Robert Browning and Elizabeth Barrett exchanged 574 letters and fell deeply in love. Their profound passion and artistic kinship prevailed over all obstacles, including Barrett's frail health and her father's strenuous objections to the union. On September 12, 1846, Robert Browning and Elizabeth Barrett secretly wed. Their marriage was, by all accounts, every bit as poetic as their writing. The two adored one another and agreed on all matters but one: the issue of spiritualism.

Elizabeth was a believer. Having been an invalid most of her life, she perhaps *needed* to believe that something existed beyond death, which so frequently threatened to take her. In her opinion, famous mediums of the day were providing incontrovertible proof. She once declared, "Skeptics have said, 'Let me see a table move, and I will believe anything.' Now the table moves, all Europe witnessing." To her dismay, her husband was among those who remained unmoved by séance the-atrics. Robert Browning viewed spiritualism as little more than sophisticated superstition and did not hesitate to say so. This difference of opinion between husband and wife was never more obvious or more public than in 1855, following what was perhaps the most famous séance of the century—an event that eventually came to be known simply as "the Browning Circle."

During the summer of that year, the famed medium Daniel Dunglas Home was the houseguest of a wealthy London solicitor named John Rymer. On July 23, several people were invited to a séance at Ealing Villa, the Rymer home. Among those invited were Elizabeth Barrett Browning, who had once announced that Home was the most interesting person in England, and her skeptical husband Robert.

Robert Browning later admitted that he was put off by Home's effusive manner before the séance even began. As the medium mingled with the guests, he referred to Mr. and Mrs. Rymer as "Mama" and "Papa." He flattered them constantly and kissed them abundantly, a display that Browning later described as being unmanly and in poor taste. Fortunately for the uncomfortable poet, the social part of the evening did not last long. By 9 PM, all 14 people present were seated at a large, round table, which was draped with a cloth and had a single lit oil lamp set at its center. The séance was about to begin.

The participants had to wait only moments before the large table seemingly came to life, vibrating and tilting of its own accord. A series of raps were then heard—according to Home, they were communication from the spirit of the Rymer's son, Wat, who had died three years earlier at the age of 12. Wat Rymer "spoke" to his grieving parents for a period of time, then communicated directly with Home.

"The spirit has pointed out five people who must leave the room," he announced. The small group of disappointed sitters left, as requested. Nine people remained in the circle, including the Brownings.

The séance resumed as the table began to move—more dramatically than it had the first time. It reared up like an animal, at one point tilting at such a great angle that the participants were amazed that the oil lamp did not go crashing to the floor. Robert Browning admitted to being mystified, later saying that "all hands were visible." When the table finally grew still, the rapping sounds began once more. Then, suddenly, the Rymers gasped in unison.

"I can feel the spirit touching me," said Mrs. Rymer.

"I feel it too," said Mr. Rymer. "It's Wat, I am sure."

The next to receive some physical attention from the spirits was Elizabeth Barrett Browning. As she sat with her hands upon the table, she and Robert were both astonished to see a fold of her skirt begin to lift upward, as though guided by a hand or object beneath the fabric. Even the skeptical Robert was baffled, admitting that there was no way an instrument of any sort could have been placed beneath his wife's skirt without her knowledge. As he pondered the mysterious phenomenon, it took place a second time. The fabric of Elizabeth's dress was tugged upwards, as if by invisible hands.

Next, one spirit announced through more rapping that it would entertain the group.

"It will play the accordion for us," said Home. "And if we put out the light, the spirit will allow Mr. Browning to see its hand."

The lamp was extinguished. The room became black, save for the dim moonlight that barely illuminated the window that led to the garden. Robert Browning later said that he could distinguish something if it passed in front of the thin muslin curtains, but that nothing at the table was visible. Then, suddenly, in this inky darkness, a glowing white hand appeared at the edge of the table near Home. It reached up and then withdrew. It rose again, bringing other hands with it. For several minutes, the seemingly disembodied hands turned, flexed and otherwise displayed themselves. Eventually, the musical spirit communicated to Home that it was prepared to play. The medium held an accordion under the table with one hand. Music—clearly being played with two hands—filled the room. Elizabeth Barrett Browning later declared that the melodies were "quite beautiful." Robert Browning agreed that the playing was competent and "expressive enough" but was not convinced that it was otherworldly.

"The spirits are asking that Mrs. Browning sit next to me," Daniel Home announced once the musical recital ended. Elizabeth changed seats as requested. The moment she had done so, a pair of snow-white spiritual hands appeared out of the dark. The hands picked up a wreath of clematis that had been sitting on the table, and placed it reverently upon the poet's head. Elizabeth later wrote to her sister about the experience, saying that the hands were very beautiful and had been very close to her. Of one hand, she wrote, "It was as near to me as this hand I write with and I saw it as distinctly. I was perfectly calm! Not troubled in any way."

The "crowning" of Elizabeth Barrett Browning was the grand finale of the spiritual spectacle. Shortly thereafter, the guests were asked to leave Mr. and Mrs. Rymer alone with Daniel Home for 15 minutes. When they reentered the room, it was well lit once more. But the spirits had apparently not left. Home told Robert Browning that their invisible guests were then willing to levitate the table while he examined its underside, searching for an explanation for the phenomenon. The table rose and Browning conducted his investigation. He admitted that he could find no explanation for what he saw.

With that, the séance ended—but the public debate had just begun.

Elizabeth was convinced that she had witnessed miracles. She told people that Daniel Home was a fabulously gifted medium who had removed all doubt from her mind. Robert, quite the opposite, was more disgusted than ever with what he called an "impudent piece of imposture." Though he was never able to explain how the manifestations were created, he felt certain that they had been nothing more than theatrics. Playing on Home's middle name, "Dunglas," Browning took to referring to the medium publicly as "Dungball." At various times, he described him as a toady, a fraud, a leech and worse. Eventually, his vitriol drove him to pen a scathing, 2000-line, satirical poem about Home, entitled "Mr. Sludge, 'The Medium'." In it, a smarmy medium goes to great lengths to justify the fakery to which he admits:

> You've heard what I confess; I don't unsay
> A single word: I cheated where I could,
> Rapped with my toe-joints, set sham hands at work,
> Wrote down names weak in sympathetic ink,
> Rubbed odic lights with ends of phosphor-match,
> And all the rest...

Robert and Elizabeth Barrett Browning would never see eye to eye on the subject of spiritualism. For the sake of domestic tranquillity, they chose not to discuss or debate the matter in private. Publicly, however, their differing opinions were well known.

Six years after the famous "Browning Circle," Elizabeth Barrett Browning finally succumbed to her persistent ill health. She died in her husband's arms, uttering her famous last words, "It is beautiful." If Robert Browning found no comfort in the concept of spiritualism, perhaps he found some in the final line of his wife's best-loved poem, the 43rd of her *Sonnets from the Portuguese*. In answer to her own famous poetic question, "How do I love thee?" Elizabeth delivered a promise:

I shall but love thee better after death.

On some level, Robert Browning must have believed it. He lived for 28 more years and chose never to remarry.

# Nathaniel Hawthorne

Nathaniel Hawthorne is considered to be one of the originators of the American short story. He spent his writing life employing what his fellow author and friend Herman Melville defined as "the power of blackness." His choice of gothic motifs could be attributed, in part, to his nature—Hawthorne suffered from brooding melancholia and recurrent, crippling depressions—but he was no doubt also influenced by a number of strange experiences. For example, the writer claimed throughout his life to see ghosts, even believing the house he lived in to be haunted. Still, the spirit he encountered most frequently was not in his home, but in the comfortable reading room of the Boston Athenaeum.

The year was 1842, and Hawthorne was a regular visitor to the reading room. He was surprised one day to learn that another man who frequented the room as often as he, the Reverend Doctor Thaddeus Harris, had recently died. He was particularly surprised because he was quite certain that he had seen the elderly gentleman in his usual chair by the fire that very day.

The following morning, Hawthorne returned to the Athenaeum. When he entered the reading room, he decided to see who was seated in Harris' chair. The writer felt an icy chill settle over him when he saw that the chair was occupied by Harris himself. Hawthorne said nothing but found a place to sit where he could carefully observe the ghost.

Harris appeared to Hawthorne in death exactly as he had in life. He read the *Boston Post*, enjoyed the warmth of

*Nathaniel Hawthorne often wrote about the supernatural and experienced strange events regularly in his everyday life.*

the fire and spoke to no one. Hawthorne was convinced that the apparition was Harris, but noted that none of the reverend's friends appeared to be aware of him. The writer seemed to be the only one who could see the ghost.

And so it was, day after day, for nearly six weeks.

As the days and weeks passed, Hawthorne considered several methods of testing his perception, but he ultimately rejected them all. He later wrote that he may have been "loath to destroy the illusion, and to rob [himself] of so good a ghost story, which might probably have been explained in some very commonplace way." Aside from that, it would have been very difficult for Hawthorne to verify the spirit's presence without addressing him directly or questioning someone else in the room. Neither action would have been appropriate, as the reading room had very strict rules forbidding conversation. Etiquette of the day would also have made it awkward to speak with the ghost because, as Hawthorne later pointed out, he "had never been introduced to Dr. Harris." Apparently he did not consider the exceptional circumstances to be sufficient excuse for a show of bad manners.

Hawthorne later reported that at some point during the six-week period when he observed Harris' ghost, it appeared to take an interest in him as well. The writer felt that the spirit might have singled him out to receive a message from the other side, but no such message was ever delivered. In fact, nothing else of interest happened. If there ever were other details rounding out the story, they have not survived the years.

In a strange way, the incompleteness of the tale makes it all the more credible: if an author of Nathaniel Hawthorne's caliber had unconsciously produced such a story from his imagination, surely he would have concocted a more satisfying conclusion.

# Guy de Maupassant

Many consider Guy de Maupassant the greatest French short-story writer ever. He was famous in Victorian times for his horror fiction, composed of dark settings, unhappy characters and nightmarish situations. Sadly, the dismal world he created with pen and paper was likely inspired by his own depressing circumstances. Maupassant had contracted syphilis in his youth and suffered from a deteriorating mental state. At one point, he began to believe that he was regularly visited by his own phantom double. In a letter to his friend Paul Bourget, he wrote:

> Every other time I come home, I see my double. I open my door, and I see him in my armchair. I know it for a hallucination, even while experiencing it. Curious! If I didn't have a little common sense, I'd be afraid.

Despite his instability, during the 1880s a prolific Maupassant wrote a volume of verse, three travel books, six novels and more than 300 short stories. Of these, a story called "The Horla" may be one of his most disturbing. Many scholars believe that the tale—one of an evil spirit that exists both within a man and independently of him, eventually driving him insane—indicated the onset of Maupassant's most severe state of madness. But others believe Maupassant's own explanation: that the story had come to him by supernatural means.

The year was 1885. Guy de Maupassant was locked in his study, attempting to write a short story, but the words would not come. He was suffering severely from writer's block. Maupassant later told friends that he was at his most desperate hour when someone appeared in the doorway. The man entered the room and sat down in a chair opposite the author. Maupassant was astounded that anyone had been able to gain entrance to the locked room, and he was *more* astounded when he recognized the mysterious person as his own phantom double. But there was little time to sit in a state of shock—almost immediately, the figure began to dictate the words of a story. Maupassant picked up his pen and began to take down the tale. At a certain point, the specter disappeared, leaving the writer to do his own work. By then, the writer's block was gone, and Maupassant worked feverishly to finish the work that his double had started.

"The Horla" was published in 1887. Only a few years later, Guy de Maupassant lost his sanity entirely. In January 1893, at the age of 42, the great writer died by his own hand in a sanitarium. We may never know whether he was haunted by mental illness or by a genuine *doppelgänger*, a phantom double who helped him to write one of the most frightening tales of all time.

# Charles Dickens

Charles Dickens may be best known for his Ghosts of Christmas Past, Present and Future, but he wrote about ghosts and the supernatural on many occasions. Though his interest was no doubt cultivated by a nanny who simultaneously entertained and terrorized him with penny dreadful–style tales, Dickens' ghosts tended to be either humorous or symbolic in nature. In person, he was known to be as skeptical as his character Ebenezer Scrooge, who at first dismissed the spectral Marley as being nothing more than "an undigested bit of beef." Yet it is known that Dickens brushed up against the paranormal at least once in his lifetime.

In 1861, Dickens wrote a tale that was published with three others under the title "Four Ghost Stories" in the periodical *All the Year Round*. It was a fictional account of a portrait painter who meets a young woman on a train. The date is September 13. They talk pleasantly for a while, then the woman asks the artist if it is possible to paint a person's portrait from memory. He is not certain, but supposes that it may be possible. She then asks him to study her face, stating that he someday "may have to take a likeness of [her]." The artist studies the young woman's features before they part company.

Two years later, a society gentleman visits the painter and asks him to paint a portrait of his deceased daughter based on nothing more than a description. The artist tries and fails several times. Finally, he uses his memory of the young woman on the train as inspiration. The client takes one look at the portrait and is elated.

> Instantly a bright look of recognition and pleasure lighted up the father's face, and he exclaimed, "That is she!"

The artist then asks when it was that the girl died. The father tells him:

> "Two years ago; on the 13th of September."

*All the Year Round* had been on sale for only a few days when Dickens received an angry letter from a real portrait painter who claimed that the author had stolen an unpublished story that he had written, which was based upon an astonishing experience that had happened to him. Each detail was identical—from the meeting on the train to the father's request for a portrait of his dead daughter. The artist felt that somehow Dickens had to have seen his own story. Otherwise, he wrote, "How else was it possible that the date, the 13th of September, could have been got at? For I never told the date until I wrote it."

Dickens was particularly astounded at that information. According to the book *Phantom Encounters* (Time-Life Books, 1988), he later said that his own story had no particular date, until he read it over and realized the importance of it having one. At that point, choosing at random, he wrote down the exact date—"September 13"—in the margin of the proof.

*Like his character Ebenezer Scrooge, Charles Dickens considered ghosts to be nothing more than a "humbug."*

Though Charles Dickens was admittedly perplexed by that event, there is nothing to suggest that he changed his fundamental disdain for spiritualists and disbelief in ghosts. At least, not during his lifetime. After his death— that is another story.

Dickens only attempted to write one mystery novel. Entitled *The Mystery of Edwin Drood*, it was to be first published in 12 instalments in a monthly magazine. In his contract with the magazine, Dickens insisted on a clause that would provide for payment to his heirs in the event of his death. It was the first time he had ever made such a request—and it may have been based on premonition. In 1870, Dickens was only six parts into his intriguing mystery when he died, leaving no notes and countless readers who were desperate to know how the Edwin Drood story was meant to conclude. It was a mystery, it seemed, that would never be solved.

Except, perhaps, by way of *another* mystery...

In Brattleboro, Vermont, approximately one year after Charles Dickens died, a young man named Thomas P. James rented a room in the home of an elderly woman who was an avid spiritualist. James had no particularly strong interest in spiritualism, but he did attend the odd séance that was hosted by his landlady. He seemed rather unaffected by this exposure until one day, when he announced to his landlady that he had been contacted by the spirit of Charles Dickens. The late author, James claimed, had chosen to work through him to complete his unfinished mystery novel.

The landlady was sincerely impressed. If the great Dickens wished to use young Thomas P. James as his writing instrument, she would do what she could to facilitate the arrangement. She granted James free room and board until the project was complete.

It took nearly a year.

In that time, there were many who witnessed James "at work." He would slump in a chair in his room, in trances that could last for several hours. When he came out of a trance, he would then write feverishly, putting down on paper every word that Dickens' spirit had told him. He was not writing, he insisted to anyone who witnessed the phenomenon. He was merely transcribing.

James' conclusion of *The Mystery of Edwin Drood* hit the book stands on October 31, 1873. Some people had heard of its coming and cried "fraud" before ever reading a word of it. Upon closer inspection, however, even the greatest literary experts were forced to admit that they were baffled. Though it seemed impossible, the final six chapters of the work read exactly as the first six had. They were identical in style. One newspaper admitted that "James could not have written this book without help from Dickens—be it spiritual or otherwise we do not know."

More than 50 years after the fact, Sir Arthur Conan Doyle took it upon himself to investigate the mysterious case. His findings were summarized in Frank Edwards' book, *Stranger Than Science* (Ace Star Books, 1959):

In the December 1927 issue of the *Fortnightly Review,* Doyle reports that James showed no literary talent whatever, either before or after that one manuscript. His education ended at the age of 13 when he had completed a course comparable to the fifth grade in the average public school. Yet, somehow, James had acquired the style and vocabulary and thinking processes of the great Charles Dickens—inexplicable accomplishments for a poorly educated employee of an American printing shop. Sir Arthur Conan Doyle concludes: "If it be indeed a parody it has the rare merit among parodies of never accentuating or exaggerating the peculiarities of the original."

Thomas P. James never did anything newsworthy after the publication of the conclusion to Dickens' mystery. He died in obscurity. Still, today a few copies of what is known as "the James version" of *The Mystery of Edwin Drood* exist. They are rare and are often billed as "an unusual Dickens item."

Unusual, indeed.

Rare, indeed.

It is seldom that an author is forced to "ghostwrite" his own work from beyond the grave.

# 4
# A Selection
# of Shades

*~*

*Perhaps because they held
such an intense interest
in spirits, the Victorians
went to great pains to
record their personal
expriences with
the paranormal. We should
be grateful that they did,
because a wealth of stories
now exists,
documenting real-life
encounters with
19th-century shades...*

*~*

# The Croglin Vampire

From the penny-dreadful adventures of *Varney the Vampire* to Bram Stoker's elegant *Dracula,* Victorians loved a toothsome tale of the undead. True vampire accounts were more difficult to dig up, however—unless you lived in Britain's scenic hills of Cumberland, near the ancient house known as Croglin Low Hall. There, in the summer of 1875, an actual vampire was said to be on the hunt.

The details are fantastic but fairly well documented. The story has been told several times, but all versions of it remain true to the original. And for those who point out a certain similarity between the characteristic signs of the Croglin Vampire and those of Count Dracula, it is worth noting that this event took place more than two decades before the publication of Stoker's famous novel.

It all began in 1875, on the evening of a summer day that had been suffocating in its heat.

For some months previous, Croglin Low Hall had been leased by three adult siblings: Edward, Michael and Amelia Cranswell. They were cultured, well-traveled, intelligent young people who had made themselves quite popular in their short time living in the area. They were also sophisticated, not prone to superstition and not believers in the supernatural. But on the evening of that sweltering day, they would be terrified into a new way of thinking.

Amelia found herself unable to sleep that night because the heat in her bedroom was so oppressive. She longed for a cooling breeze. Because the bedrooms were at ground level, Edward had insisted from the time that they moved in that all of the windows be securely latched at night. Still, the air was *so* stifling that Amelia decided that leaving the window fastened while opening the heavy wooden shutters would be a reasonable compromise.

It was an unusually beautiful night. The moon was high and full, and it bathed the expansive lawn in exquisite, silver light. Amelia lay propped against her pillows, gazing out the window at the magical view. After a while, she noticed something quite curious.

In the distance, along the belt of trees that surrounded the neighboring church, she detected two pinpoints of yellow light. Amelia watched, fascinated for several minutes as the twin orbs repeatedly vanished and reappeared amongst the trees. Then the lights began to move. Amelia realized that they were traveling at great speed toward the house, *toward her window*. Startled, she sat up in bed and wondered what to do.

She had to alert her brothers. She leapt from her bed, grabbed the key to her bedroom door and fumbled in the dark trying to unlock it. As she tried to fit the key in place, she heard a light, scratching noise on the window glass behind her. Amelia spun around. There, only a few feet away from her were the two flaming, yellow lights. She could see then that they were eyes, set in a wizened, brown face that was pressed up against the window. It was horrifying. It was hideous. And it was scratching again at the glass.

Amelia forced herself to look away, to work more fervently at getting the key in the lock. But her hands were trembling so violently that she dropped it. It went clattering away on the floor, hopelessly lost in the inky black

*The window through which the vampire entered was bricked up long ago and covered with horseshoes for luck.*

shadows. Amelia felt terror swelling inside her as she realized that she was locked in the room.

At that moment, the scratching stopped. In its place, there came an insistent pecking sound. The creature—whatever it was—was picking away at the lead that held the glass in place. Amelia realized that the thing with the vile yellow eyes would use whatever means and force necessary to gain entrance to her room. With this knowledge, she found her voice and began to scream.

Scream after scream issued from her, and she could soon hear her brothers stumbling about in the darkened hallway, running into the walls and each other as they made their way to her room. But the door remained locked, and as they pounded helplessly on it, there was a tinkling sound as a diamond-shaped pane of glass, picked free of its lead, fell into the room. A long, thin, claw-like hand slipped through the opening and undid the window latch. In an instant it was undone, and the window swung open. The creature—whose entire being was as rail-thin and bony as its hand—threw one long leg over the sill and entered the room.

Mercifully, Amelia recalled little of what happened next. Her memory held only a collection of snapshot images: the burning yellow eyes, advancing; a repulsive, skeletally thin figure towering over her; the menacing, claw-like hands reaching for her...

Unconsciousness came as a sweet, welcome relief.

On the other side of the bedroom door, Edward and Michael Cranswell pounded helplessly as they listened to the sounds of their sister's gruesome attack. Finally, after they had thrown themselves against it many times, the heavy door gave way. The brothers burst into the room to find Amelia bleeding profusely on the floor, having suffered numerous slashes and punctures to her face, throat and shoulders. Michael noticed the open window at once, and rushed over in time to see his sister's attacker racing across the lawn. Michael leapt over the sill and ran in hot pursuit of the escapee, but to no avail. The tall figure seemed capable of impossibly long strides and was soon lost beyond the tree line near the churchyard. Frustrated, Michael returned to the house to help his injured sister.

For two days, they did not know if Amelia would live or die. When finally she rallied, her brothers felt huge relief—but also a great need to bring her assailant to justice. The problem was not knowing who or what had attacked her.

"These wounds could have been made by a large dog," the doctor observed.

"But we heard no growling," protested Michael.

"And what dog is capable of picking the lead from window glass?" snorted Edward. There were no clues and no suspects. It seemed at first that the offender would indefinitely remain at large.

Some weeks later, a local farmer paid a visit to Croglin Low Hall.

"I know you've had some trouble," he said to the Cranswell brothers. "I think it's the same sort of trouble that I've had in the past. I thought I might talk to you about it."

Edward and Michael invited the man in and listened to his incredible story. The farmer said that there had been an intruder in his own home some two years before, and that whoever it was had attacked his own little daughter in the same vicious way that Amelia Cranswell had been attacked.

"She was bitten o'er her face and neck and shoulders," he said. "She'll never look right again. And she's never been able to describe the fiend that did it."

What was more, the farmer told the Cranswells that there were other houses where women had awakened to a terrifying sight.

"They seen a terrible monster, one shaped like a man, trying to get in where they was. But those women, they screamed out in time. Not like my girl or your sister."

The Cranswells did not know what to think, but they did agree with one another that it would be best if they took Amelia to Switzerland to recuperate. By September, however, she insisted that they return home. She felt certain that she would be safe.

"After all," she said, "lunatics don't escape every day."

The brothers finally acquiesced, and all three Cranswells returned to Croglin Low Hall. The sleeping arrangements were changed: Edward and Michael moved their beds into a room that was directly across the hall from Amelia's. They kept two loaded pistols by their door and insisted that their sister keep her shutters closed and her door unlocked.

The winter passed uneventfully. Then came the spring, and one chilly March night when Amelia was awakened by the familiar, menacing sound of long fingernails scratching on glass. She screamed instantly. Michael ran immediately to her side, and Edward, according to the plan they had made, went charging out the front door.

Out on the lawn he saw a tall, thin creature bounding toward the trees. Edward raised his pistol and fired. He hit his mark. The being stumbled for a few steps before regaining its balance. It carried on, but at a slower pace. Edward gave chase, certain that he could overtake the injured thing.

As before, the tall figure ran toward the belt of trees. Edward followed. The creature ducked into the shadows of the tangled branches. Again, Edward followed. He emerged on the other side, in time to see the intruder limping toward the 20-foot wall that surrounded the churchyard. He watched in astonishment as the inhuman thing effortlessly crept up the side of the wall and scrambled over the top. Edward raced around to the front gates, praying all the while that he would not lose sight of his quarry. He got there just in time to see a tall, sinister shadow slipping through the doors of the cemetery's largest vault.

By the first light of day, Edward and Michael Cranswell had gathered a group of men together. They carried lanterns and pistols and wore grim expressions as they made their way silently to the cemetery. Once there, they passed by rows upon rows of crumbling tombstones. Most of the names etched on those stones were familiar: they were the names of family members, loved ones and neighbors. But the men were not there to pay respects, so they did not stop until they reached the rusted doors of the largest tomb.

"It was through here that I saw him vanish," said Edward.

The others nodded solemnly. Two of the strongest men then went to work on the doors, prying at the thick cables of iron chain that held them fast. Finally, two links broke. With some coaxing from a pry bar, the doors swung open. The tortured groan of the corroded hinges echoed down into the vault.

"Who's with us, then?"

The Cranswell brothers stood together at the opening of the tomb, their pistols drawn and ready. After a moment's hesitation, three of the other men stepped forward to join them. Each one of the five then took a lantern in one hand and a weapon in the other and descended, single-file, into the dank gloom of the vault.

The screaming began within seconds.

The men waiting in the cemetery watched in horror as the first of their friends reemerged from the darkness. The man was babbling incoherently, howling and shrieking in terror. Before they could ask him what he had seen, he broke away from them and bolted out of the churchyard. The other men might have followed him, if the Cranswell brothers and their two remaining supporters had not emerged from the tomb at that moment.

"We'll be needing wooden stakes," said Edward, "and wood for a funeral pyre."

The men who had remained above ground stared at him in astonishment.

"Surely not!" said one.

"You can't have found more than a criminal's hiding place!" said another.

But the Cranswells told them otherwise. The chamber had been strewn with the wreckage of splintered coffins. The gruesome remnants of corpses were everywhere. And, in the midst of it all, one coffin stood untouched. Inside of it lay the body of a tall, grotesquely thin man with a shriveled brown face and claw-like hands. He was dressed in the fashions of another century, yet his body was remarkably well preserved. The men were examining the corpse's peculiarly long, curved teeth when they

*The cemetery at Croglin Church is the alleged location of the Croglin vampire's grave.*

noticed a dark liquid streaming from the corners of the man's mouth. When they held a lantern close they could see that it was fresh, red blood.

"This is no lunatic," said Edward. "Nor is it a criminal. What we have here, attacking our women in the night...is a vampire."

Those who had ventured into the tomb were convinced. Those who had waited in the churchyard were inclined to believe their friends. But any doubt that may have lingered in anyone's mind was banished some hours later in the full light of day when the corpse was brought above ground and staked through the heart. For it was then, before throwing the skeletal figure on the flaming pyre, that Edward took note of a peculiar hole in its ragged trousers.

"Wait a moment," he commanded, as he tore the cloth away from the body. Beneath the trouser leg, he saw a similar hole in the dry, mummified flesh. Fighting his revulsion, he thrust his index finger into the wound. After a moment, he extracted something.

It was a pistol ball. Quite a unique pistol ball, of unusual coloring.

"That's the ammunition you bought in Switzerland!" Michael gasped.

Edward nodded. He remembered making the purchase the previous summer, while Amelia lay recovering from her first attack. At the time, he did not imagine that he would be using that same ammunition to help bring down her attacker, or, for that matter, that her attacker would prove to be something so vile and unholy as the monster that lay before him at that moment.

Edward stood up.

"Now," he said.

All the men bent down and took hold of the corpse. Together, with one heaving motion, they tossed it on the flames. Then they watched as the fire took what remained of the vampire of Croglin Low Hall.

# The Nurse

In the year 1870, in Victorian England, Patricia Clancy was 10 years old and her brother Christopher was 11. They were vacationing with their parents in the popular seaside resort of Scarborough that summer when they experienced something so rare and unusual that they would remember it for the rest of their lives. The event was documented in John Macklin's book, *Dwellers in Darkness* (Ace Books, 1968), and it is the basis of this tale.

It was a pleasant afternoon, and the youngsters were amusing themselves by the water's edge, feeding the swans bits of bread left over from the sandwiches they had eaten for lunch. Mr. and Mrs. Clancy relaxed on a park bench a short distance away, enjoying the sunshine and sea air as they watched their children at play.

After a time, a young woman in a nurse's uniform joined Patricia and Christopher. She had with her a paper bag filled with broken biscuits, which she began feeding to the birds. Since the children had used up all of their bread crusts by the time the nurse arrived, they turned their attention to her.

"Lovely day," said the nurse with a smile.

The children needed no further encouragement. They launched into a long line of chatter about the swans and the weather and the boarding house near Peasholme Park where they were staying. The nurse then asked them where they were from, and did they attend school there, and did they have any other brothers or sisters. The children answered each query excitedly, and in rambling detail, sometimes stepping on each other's sentences in their eagerness to explain some tidbit or another.

At one point, Patricia paused.

"I suppose we shouldn't talk your ear off," she said, although it was clear from her expression that she wished to continue.

"Don't be silly," laughed the nurse. "I enjoy the company of children—much more than that of adults, I must say. Perhaps it's because I worked for so long in the children's ward at the hospital here," she said.

Patricia cocked her head to one side and knit her brow.

"Don't you work there anymore?" she asked.

The nurse didn't answer. She did not even appear to have heard Patricia's question, as she was looking over the girl's shoulder, focusing intently upon something in the distance. Her pretty features twisted into an anxious mask.

"Be careful!" she shrieked suddenly. "Be careful—you could fall in! The currents are strong here! You could be swept away!"

Patricia turned around, following the nurse's frightened gaze. She spotted Christopher at the edge of the pier, poised to dip one bare foot into the water. He looked sheepish but confused, as though he had no idea what he had done wrong.

"I only wanted to splash a bit with my toes," he explained. "And look, you can see the bottom here. It's only a few feet down."

"But it's *very dangerous*," insisted the nurse. Her eyes had grown as dark as thunderclouds, and jagged patches of high color appeared on her cheeks. "*Very dangerous, indeed!*"

Patricia and Christopher looked at each other uneasily. They weren't accustomed to being chastised by strangers, let alone for such an innocuous offense. They were relieved a moment later to hear their father calling them back to the bench.

"Nice to meet you," the children mumbled in polite unison as they turned to leave. The young nurse did not appear to hear them. She was staring out over the water, fretfully wringing her hands.

Christopher was worried that he might receive a second dressing-down from his parents, so he began laying out his defense before they could say a word.

"I *was* being careful by the water," he said. "You know I always am. That nurse was very nice to talk to but, if you ask me, she was on the panicky side."

Patricia nodded in agreement, but Mr. and Mrs. Clancy only looked at each other with confused expressions.

"What nurse?" they said in unison.

It was the children's turn to appear confused.

"That lady, in the nurse's uniform," said Patricia. "She was right there with us for the longest time. We were chatting. Surely you saw her?"

But Mr. and Mrs. Clancy insisted that they had not. *Such imaginations,* they were thinking as they gazed at their children.

*How unobservant!* Christopher and Patricia silently marveled as they looked up at their parents.

But the matter was not spoken of again until the following afternoon, when Patricia suffered an accident.

The girl was playing in the waves near the shore when she was stung by some sea creature that didn't want to share its watery home with splashing, rowdy children. Her foot and leg began to swell so much that her parents thought it best to seek medical treatment. They packed her off to the local hospital. Christopher, disappointed that his afternoon of play had been disrupted, trailed sulkily along with them.

Once at the hospital, Mr. and Mrs. Clancy sat in the waiting room with Christopher while Patricia was tended to in a curtained cubicle by a friendly young nurse named Rose Wilton. It wasn't long before the little girl was feeling much better. As she improved, she became more of her spirited, curious self. She began to ask Nurse Wilton endless questions about her job. The young nurse answered them all with patient good cheer.

"You know," said Patricia, "you're the second nurse I've met on this holiday. My brother and I were talking with a very nice lady yesterday. She said she used to work here. *Exactly* here, in fact, in the children's ward."

"It must have been some time ago," said Nurse Wilton. "We've had no staff changes for several years."

Patricia looked doubtful.

"Couldn't have been too long ago," she said. "She was a young lady—like you."

Rose Wilton blanched a little, and the expression of patient amusement faded from her face.

"Wait just a moment," she said to Patricia. "I have to fetch something."

When Nurse Wilton returned, she was clutching a faded photograph. She showed it to Patricia, whose face lit up with recognition.

"That's her!" she said, brightly. "That's the nurse we met!"

"I thought it might be," Rose Wilton said. But her voice was serious and her smile was strained and when she excused herself for the second time, Patricia was wondering if she had done or said something wrong.

Mrs. Clancy was the first one to notice Nurse Wilton coming down the hall toward the waiting room. She saw how the color had drained out of her cheeks and the smile had left her eyes.

"Nothing's wrong, I hope?" she asked anxiously when Rose Wilton entered the room.

"Wrong? No, no, not at all," Nurse Wilton hurriedly assured her. "Patricia's fine. Ready to go, in fact. If my manner startled you, I am sorry. I've just had a bit of a shock, you see."

She then pulled the creased photograph from the pocket of her uniform and showed it to Mr. and Mrs. Clancy.

"I realize that this may seem an odd question," she began, "but have you ever seen this woman?"

Mr. Clancy shook his head.

"No. Never," said Mrs. Clancy.

"I have!" said Christopher. He had come up behind his parents and was peering through the space that separated them at Rose Wilton's tattered photograph. "That's the nurse! The one we met yesterday while feeding the swans!"

"I saw no one with you yesterday," Mr. Clancy said in a stern voice. He believed that it was one thing for a child to weave fantastic stories for his own amusement, but quite another to draw a stranger into the fantasy.

"But she was there!" Christopher protested.

Before Mr. or Mrs. Clancy could say another word, Rose Wilton stepped in.

"You may both be right," she said. "This is a photo of my friend—my best friend. Patricia also identified her as the nurse she met yesterday."

"Yes, she was very nice," said Christopher. "Easily upset, though. She got herself quite worked up when I stepped near the water's edge."

"Well now," Nurse Wilton said thoughtfully, "that makes sense."

Mr. Clancy was growing impatient.

"It makes *no* sense!" he blustered. "This is *ridiculous!*"

But then Nurse Wilton asked Christopher if he wouldn't mind sitting down for a moment, because she needed to talk to his parents in private.

"Adult business," she said, giving him a conspiratorial wink. "Very dull, you understand."

She then led Mr. and Mrs. Clancy around the corner into the hall. There, in whispers, she explained herself.

"I think it's quite possible that your children met my friend yesterday," she said. "And I think it's equally possible that you did not notice her presence. You see, my friend..." she paused for a moment and looked behind her to confirm that Christopher was still well out of earshot. "My friend was always very fond of children. Very concerned for their safety."

"Be that as it may—" began Mr. Clancy.

"She died four summers ago," Rose Wilton said then.

The Clancys stared at her in shock.

"I believed the children when they identified her in the picture, but what convinced me thoroughly was Christopher describing her agitation when he was at the water's edge."

"Why was that?" asked Mrs. Clancy in a voice as dry as sand.

"Because of how she died," said Nurse Wilton. "My friend drowned, you see. She was trying to save a child who had been swept out to sea by the current."

"How terrible," muttered Mr. Clancy. He shook his head in a sympathetic way.

"Yes," agreed Rose Wilton. "It was very tragic." She tucked the photo carefully back into her pocket. Then, almost as an afterthought, she added something more.

"It was only by chance that she was even there," she said. "It was only because she had a few broken biscuits that she wanted to feed the swans..."

# The Screaming Skeleton

It had become as predictable as the setting of the sun.

Every night at the same hour, a woman named Mrs. Fox would usher out her last customer, close the doors of the small tavern she operated and go upstairs to the cramped rooms where she and her family lived. She would check on her children, who had been tucked into their beds hours earlier, and prepare to retire. But when she slipped beneath the covers, she would find herself too agitated to close her eyes. And so she would stare grimly at the ceiling until the screaming began.

She never had to wait long.

The year was 1860, the place was Sedgley in the West Midlands of England and rumors were spreading far and wide about the Fox family's Pig and Whistle Pub. In truth, people had been whispering about the pub long before Mrs. Fox and her brood moved in and took over operations; there were stories that went back several years, through several different proprietors and tenants. No one ever stayed long at the Pig and Whistle. No one could put up with the inhuman wailing.

"At first, frightened as I was, I tried to follow the sound," Mrs. Fox once confided to a friend. "It seemed to come from the fireplace." Others corroborated her story—sensible, intelligent folks who knew that a fireplace could not scream. And yet that is what so many terrified witnesses had heard—piercing, unspeakable cries that seemingly originated in the cooling ashes of the hearth. It was an unsolvable mystery, until Mrs. Fox decided that she too had been tormented long enough.

Sometime during the summer months, Mrs. Fox packed up her children and her belongings and vacated the premises. It was then that the landlord discovered that Mrs. Fox had been the last person willing to take up tenancy in the old pub. For a time, the windows were boarded up and the doors were nailed firmly shut, as though the tavern was waiting patiently for its next occupants. But when it became obvious that there was no one else brave enough or ignorant enough to pay rent for the privilege of being mercilessly haunted, the landlord came to a decision. The old Pig and Whistle would be torn down and rebuilt. It would be a cathartic process that would surely rid the premises of its screaming spirit.

Workmen were brought in. Timbers were pulled down, and stones were dislodged. Before the deconstruction was complete, the men on the job made a discovery that was described by the newspapers of the day as being "so appalling that it has drawn thousands of people to the scene." Besides shocking the townspeople, the appalling discovery also happened to solve the mystery: buried beneath the hearthstone, which had long been considered the source of the spectral screaming, the workmen found a portion of a human skeleton.

No one knew how long the pitiful bones had lain there, but at long last people felt that they knew the reason for the ghostly keening that had long been haunting the Pig and Whistle Pub.

# The Gray Lady of Hackwood

An eerie story took place in the 1860s, involving a certain gentleman and the famous shadowy specter known to haunt a grand home near Basingstoke in Hampshire.

The man—an analytical, skeptical sort—was one of several guests staying at Hackwood Hall on this occasion. On the evening of the first day, as he prepared to go to sleep, he was startled by what appeared to be a ghost.

It was a gray shape, misty and ethereal, that appeared to drift out of the bedroom wall. The man watched in amazement as the vaporous cloud began to coalesce into the figure of a woman. She remained shadowy and transparent, but her cloak, streaming hair and mournful features were plainly visible. She longingly reached out her hand toward the astonished man and then, in the blink of an eye, vanished.

For several moments, he remained in shock. When his heart stopped pounding, his logical mind went to work.

"It's a prank of some sort," he muttered to himself. "The others have decided to have a good laugh at my expense." He imagined that the other guests were waiting at the bottom of the stairs, stifling their laughter, waiting for him to run screaming out of his room. Determined to disappoint them, he instead went to work examining the area of the room where the murky image had appeared. He ran his fingers over the walls, tipped the heavy pieces of furniture and swept the cobwebs from behind the pictures and ornaments. Yet he could find nothing to explain what he had seen.

"So, it's sophisticated trickery," he concluded. "But it's trickery, none the less."

He extinguished the lamp on his bedside table and crawled beneath the covers. Before he was able to close his eyes and drift off to sleep, a small movement at the foot of the bed caught his attention.

It was the gray mist once more. This time, in the darkness, the man was able to discern a dull, pulsating glow at its core. But, aside from the sickly light, all was the same. The shadows swirled and thickened, eventually forming the phantom shape of a woman. The wraith stared at the man with soulless, unseeing eyes and reached out toward him. Then, in an instant, she was gone.

The man did not require a third encounter to convince him that the ghost was real. He hid under his covers for the remainder of the night, praying that she would not return.

The next morning, he was feeling more himself—and once again he was doubting that he had been visited by a genuine apparition. Fearing ridicule from his fellow house guests, he resolved to say nothing of his frightening nighttime adventure. He arrived at the breakfast table carefully composed, determined that neither his appearance nor his conversational tone would betray his secret.

Despite his efforts to seem casual, the other guests appeared more interested in him than in each other. Every time he spoke, they turned their attention fully toward him, as though they expected him to say something far more interesting than "Please pass the butter." Eventually, their behavior aggravated him to the point where he was forced to say something.

"Is there something the matter?" he asked, in an irritated tone. "Have I committed some terrible *faux pas,* or did I dribble jelly on my sleeve? There must be some reason you're all staring at me."

Several people at the table cleared their throats uncomfortably. A few stared down at their plates. One woman finally spoke.

"I am sorry if we've made you uncomfortable," she said. "It's just that we're curious. We know you don't put much stock in spooks and spirits, but we would like to know what happened."

"What happened? What do you mean, 'what happened?'" the man said defensively.

The woman looked uncomfortable, but pressed further.

"I feel foolish asking...It's just that we *all* saw it, and we're now wondering—"

The man set his teacup down with such force that it rattled the saucer.

"So you admit it then!" he thundered. "The lot of you are to blame for what happened last night!"

"Blame!" said the woman. "We did nothing! We only saw—"

"You saw, you saw—you saw *what?*" the man demanded.

All of the house guests were staring at him now. The woman who had been speaking had patches of color blooming in her cheeks. She had begun to pick nervously at the lace collar of her dress. But there was determination in her eyes, and she lifted her chin boldly when she spoke.

"We all watched you as you walked up the staircase to your room last night," she said. "And we were wondering if anything strange happened to you after that."

"Anything strange!" the man spat. "Now why on earth would you ask that?"

"Because," explained the woman, "as you climbed the stairs, you were followed—by a mysterious, misty, gray shadow. It was the oddest thing, so we were interested. But forgive us for asking at all."

The man went pale then and began to tremble. It was several moments before he could speak.

"I'm sorry for having been so rude," he finally said, "but I haven't had a wink of sleep. You see, something did happen last night and I don't think I completely believed it until this minute..."

And so he told his story. The fellow house guests listened attentively, then all agreed: their friend had most certainly met the Gray Lady of Hackwood.

# A Ghostly Telegram

In the Victorian era, interest and acceptance regarding the paranormal were so great that it was commonplace to find accounts of people's personal supernatural experiences in the daily paper. Such was the case in January 1870, when several newspapers of the day picked up a small item from the Auburn *Advertiser* that told the strange story of a certain unnamed "prominent citizen."

According to the account, the man was visiting Chicago for business reasons. One evening, after a busy day of meetings, he felt particularly fatigued and decided to retire early. He returned to his hotel room and prepared for bed. But as he eased back onto the plump feather pillows and pulled the covers up to his chin, the man was startled out of his relaxed state by a sudden, frightening message.

*"Your mother died today."*

It was a human voice, plain and clear, and as loud as if the speaker had been standing beside the bed. Even more upsetting than the disembodied nature of the message was its tone of absolute assurance. The man, a sensible businessman who was not given to flights of fancy, was left with no doubt whatsoever that the sad news was true.

The man spent a sleepless, grief-filled night in his hotel room. At the first light of dawn, he dressed, packed his belongings and made immediate preparations for the journey home. He had planned to stay longer; there was more business to do, but it would have to wait. The man first had to bury his mother.

Suitcase in hand, the man walked out of the hotel. Before he had gone too far, he spotted a uniformed boy with a telegraph dispatch in his hand. Although he had no way of knowing for certain, the man strongly sensed that the message was for him. He called the boy over and, giving his name, asked if the wire message was addressed to him.

It was. And the message, of course, was identical to the one he had received by supernatural means the previous evening. The news had been confirmed: the man's mother had died the previous day in her home in Auburn.

The newspaper concluded:

> He had received no information but that she was enjoying her usual health; nor had there been anything to excite in the slightest degree his apprehension for her safety, until the occurrence of the incident related.

In other words, he had no reason to expect that he would be receiving such a sad telegram—ghostly, or otherwise.

# Quarantined with a Ghost

It was not as though the neighbors didn't warn them...

"Don't move into that house," they said. "It's haunted. No one ever stays there more than a few days..."

But the rent had been paid, and the plan to move into the Baltimore neighborhood was in place. Moreover, the husband of the house was a military man, a Civil War veteran who placed no stock in tales of the supernatural, and his wife was of a similar steadfast nature. They liked the rambling, two-story house—it had come very inexpensively and they were not about to start looking for other accommodations over a ghost story.

Not even over such a *disturbing* ghost story.

It was said that a proud Englishwoman and her two children had starved to death in the house. "She kept to herself," the neighbors said, "so we had no way of knowing the family was destitute." Instead of asking for help when her husband abandoned the family, the woman simply locked the doors and waited for the inevitable. The neighbors would often see her in one of the second-floor windows, slowly rocking in her rocking chair, watching over the tree-lined street. Eventually that was where they found her: dead, in the rocker, with the lifeless forms of her two children curled in her lap.

Afterwards, no tenant ever stayed for long and the neighbors would sometimes see a dark shadow moving rhythmically back and forth in the window—back and forth, back and forth, as though rocking.

But the veteran and his wife remained skeptical and so they moved their large family into the house.

It wasn't long before they began to question their wisdom in the matter, because the house seemed to have a decidedly unfriendly feel to it. On the staircase leading to the second floor, there was an area of icy cold that could not be explained. Anyone walking past this spot would experience a sense of resistance, a reluctance to pass by. To make matters worse, the lamp lights, no matter how carefully protected, always extinguished as they were being carried up those stairs.

But it was more than a feeling—there were sounds too. In the dark of night, the family could hear the soft, inconsolable sobbing of a woman. The floorboards would often rattle and thump, though nothing visible moved over them. And in the front bedroom on the second floor, near the window overlooking the street, evening would bring the slow insistent creaking of a wooden rocker. This sound recurred although the chair where the woman and her children had been found had long ago been taken away.

Still, the family chose to stay. Ironically, it was not long before staying was no longer a matter of choice. One of the young children became ill with typhoid fever. As a result, the family was quarantined in their haunted home, no longer able to leave of their own free will. The ghost, or ghosts, in the house seemed to sense this, and the haunting intensified. Eerie noises grew louder, the feeling of ominous oppression grew more intense and ultimately, the presence lashed out physically at the captive family.

*"What was that?"*

The sound of a loud slap interrupted the family at dinner one evening. It came from the main floor bedroom where the sick child was recuperating. It was immediately followed by the youngster's pained howling. Everyone forgot their half-eaten dinner and rushed to the bedroom to see what had happened.

"A lady hit me!" the child sobbed to his parents. They could see that he had been struck. An angry red mark in the shape of a hand had begun to form on his cheek. The mark eventually faded, but there would be other similar attacks—on two of the other sons and on the mother. The family could do nothing but suffer the assaults and pray for either the ghost to leave or the quarantine to be lifted. Not surprisingly, it was the quarantine that ended first.

The story was originally told by a descendant of the family to author Dennis Bardens for inclusion in his book *Ghosts and Hauntings* (Ace Books, 1965). According to that account, as soon as they were able, "the family moved out posthaste."

Apparently, nothing can turn skeptics into believers quite as effectively as being quarantined with a ghost.

# A Devilish Tenant

It was an average-looking little rental house on St. Mary Street in Halifax, Nova Scotia. It was so like its neighbors on the block, so utterly nondescript, that no one would have ever taken any notice of it. That is, if it hadn't been for a period of time in the summer of 1869 when the people who lived there began to claim that Satan had taken up residence in the cellar.

"The masses may laugh and jeer and sneer," one tenant told a reporter, "but if they were only here instead of us, they would soon find out the terrible truth we are telling."

That truth, according to the tenants, was that the devil himself had become their nasty downstairs neighbor. It had started one evening, they said, when the trap door leading to their cellar flew open with a crash. Before anyone even had a moment to wonder how that had happened, things began to fly out of the dark hole. There was a worn scrubbing brush, a shower of iron nails and handfuls of broken eggshells. All of this was accompanied by the powerful stench of brimstone. The eruption lasted for several seconds and concluded with the slamming shut of the trap door.

The neighbors heard the great commotion and screaming and asked the next day what had gone on. The tenants explained that the Devil had set up his infernal headquarters next to where they stored their cabbages and potatoes. Naturally, and predictably, the neighbors scoffed.

So the tenants invited them to experience His Evilness for themselves.

The following evening, several neighbors sat around in the cramped kitchen of the little house, waiting for something unspeakable to happen. Sure enough, as midnight approached, there grew a rumbling beneath the cellar trap door. Suddenly it flung open, and the darkness below began to belch out an assortment of eggshells, nails, feathers and other odds and ends. The neighbors, who had been so skeptical, ran from the house screaming. Later, one of them declared that he had dared to look down the hole, and saw the Devil there, "sitting in a corner with his tail twisted 'round his neck.'"

Days passed, and the disruption continued, with trash spewing out of the trap door at regular intervals. At one point, the police were sent for, in the hope that even Satan would bow down to the presence of the law. One officer happened to be in the house investigating when the cellar door blasted open and the usual miscellanies came shooting out.

"Do you see? Do you see?" shrieked the lady of the house.

The officer—obviously one of the bravest men ever to pin on a badge—took a good long look down into the inky depths of the cellar.

"I don't see the Devil," he finally reported, "but if I did, I would just charge you for having spirits in the house without a license."

It seemed that the police did not take the tenants' claim seriously. There were others who did not as well. One newspaper account of the devilish events concluded as follows:

A hard-headed unbeliever says that the tenant in the house has for some time found the rent rather high and is desirous to lower or have it lowered by some or any means. Surely, surely not…

# A Spirit Seeks Forgiveness

An intriguing story was once told by a Russian nobleman, Baron Basil von Driesen, in which he claimed that he shook hands with the ghost of his father-in-law only days after the man's death. The father-in-law died on November 20, 1860. Nine days later, there was to be a liturgy for the repose of his soul. It was in the early morning hours of that ninth day that the restless spirit sought out the baron.

Von Driesen had gone to bed well after midnight on that evening, and he spent some time reading the Bible before sleep. When he grew too tired to read, he snuffed out the candle flame. It was then that he heard the sound of shuffling footsteps in the adjoining room. Slowly, slowly, the shuffling grew louder, until it seemed to the baron that someone had stopped directly outside the bedroom door.

"Who is there?" Von Driesen called out. There was no answer. Determined to find out, he struck a match. The flame bloomed in the darkness, revealing the image of the baron's father-in-law standing directly in front of the bedroom door.

"Yes, it was he," Baron von Driesen would later recall. "In his blue dressing gown, lined with squirrel furs and only half-buttoned, so that I could see his white waistcoat and his black trousers."

The baron was not frightened at the appearance of the specter, but he was curious. He and his father-in-law had not been on good terms at the time of the man's death. He wondered why it was that the man's ghost had chosen to appear.

"What do you want?" the baron boldly asked.

The apparition crossed the room, stopping when he reached the baron's bedside. With a sorrowful expression, he addressed his son-in-law by name.

"I have acted wrongly toward you," the ghost then said. "Forgive me. Without this, I do not feel at rest there." He pointed heavenward with his left hand to illustrate what he meant. With his right hand, he reached out toward the baron.

"I seized this hand," remembered the baron, "which was long and cold. [I] shook it and answered, 'God is my witness that I have never had anything against you.'"

The ghost bowed and moved away from the bed. Before he was able to shuffle through the doorway, he vanished from sight. Baron von Driesen crossed himself, put out the candle once more and fell into a deep, untroubled sleep.

The following day, at the celebration of the liturgy, the priest approached the baron.

"Your father-in-law came to me just after midnight this morning," he said. He claimed that the ghost had come to ask for his help. "He was seeking a reconciliation with you, Baron," the priest said.

Newspaper accounts do not indicate how the priest assisted, or if he assisted, only that he later confirmed his part of the incredible story in a written statement that was signed and sent to the Society for Psychical Research.

# Lady Arabella

She was the lovely Lady Arabella Stuart, born in 1575 to Margaret, Queen of Scotland. He was Sir William Seymour, the second Duke of Somerset. They fell deeply in love and married in June 1610. It was a tragic union that would result in one of the most romantic ghost stories of the Victorian era.

Arabella was a descendant of Henry VII and, after James I, stood next in line for the English throne. But for her, being high-born was not the blessing one might imagine. Her proximity to the throne only caused her to be under suspicion for all of her life. King James considered her a threat to his security—a threat that was sure to intensify if Arabella was to marry. When James discovered that his royal relative was being courted by Sir William, he forbade their union—and when he learned that they had disobeyed him and married in secret, he had both of the lovers arrested. Seymour was taken to the dreaded Tower of London, and Lady Arabella was confined to the grounds of Lambeth Palace.

Ah, but it's never so easy to discourage true love.

With the help of sympathizers, William and Arabella managed to communicate. They formed a plan to escape to the Continent, but all did not go as hoped. Sir William was successful, but his wife was captured and returned to the king, who decided that her days of living luxuriously in a gilded cage were over. James I had Lady Arabella imprisoned in the tower, where she lost her sanity and eventually her life. William Seymour lived for another 45 years after Arabella's death. He died in October 1660 at the age of 73.

It was some time after that the lovers began to meet again...

More than two centuries later, a woman named Emma Petrie was working as a seamstress at Lambeth Palace, where Lady Arabella had originally been confined. One autumn day in 1864, as Mrs. Petrie was walking down a corridor in the palace, she met a lady who made a great impression upon her. She appeared dignified and well-bred but had a sorrow in her expression that seemed infinite. What truly captured Emma Petrie's attention, though, was the lady's outlandish dress, like none other that the seamstress had seen. As she was marveling at the costume, the lady swept by—and Mrs. Petrie was chilled by a bone-numbing sensation of cold. It was as if an icy breeze accompanied the mysterious woman as she moved along the hallway. But that was not as unsettling as what Emma Petrie noticed next. The story is documented in John Macklin's book, *Dwellers in Darkness:*

> She turned to look back—and to her horror she saw that the lady was not walking along the corridor but appeared to be gliding smoothly along, her feet not

touching the ground. Fear gripped Mrs. Petrie then
and she turned and hurried away.

According to Macklin's account, this encounter was the
first of several in which the seamstress met the spirit on
that day. Though she initially told no one of her experience, she began to ask questions about the history of the
palace. Within hours, she had learned the story of Lady
Arabella and Sir William and discovered that the phantom's dress, which had seemed so strange to her, had been
the fashion of Lady Arabella's day. Eventually, Mrs. Petrie
became convinced that it was the ghost of the lovelorn
lady whom she was seeing.

And she saw her again and again as the day progressed.
The second time the seamstress encountered the spirit,
she hid in a doorway for several minutes and watched as
the long-dead lady drifted up and down the corridor,
apparently searching for something. She vanished on that
occasion when she passed through a closed door. Mrs.
Petrie met the ghost for a third time in one of the palace's
grand rooms. Again, Lady Arabella was desperately seeking something. The ghost began to fade away as she
searched and then disappeared through a solid wall.

If Emma Petrie had any question who or what it was
that the ghostly lady was looking for, she did not have to
wonder for long. As the sun began to set on the seamstress' incredible day, she encountered Lady Arabella one
last time—in the palace gardens. The phantom was slipping silently along a garden pathway when she was met by
a second spectral figure. From his handsome appearance
and 17th-century costume, Mrs. Petrie judged him to be

Sir William Seymour. This impression seemed to be confirmed when the two shadowy figures joined hands and moved silently away together.

Emma Petrie would eventually learn that she was one of many witnesses to the apparitions of the star-crossed lovers. She would also learn that while Sir William was imprisoned in the Tower and Lady Arabella was confined at Lambeth Palace, sympathetic and powerful friends sometimes enabled them to meet—in the palace gardens. It was little wonder that they continued to meet in that magical location after their deaths.

In her lengthy poem "Arabella Stuart," the Romantic poet Felicia Hemans (1793–1835) sought to illustrate Lady Arabella's yearning during her imprisonment in the final years of her life. Though Hemans created a dark picture of the doomed woman's emotional state, the final line of the poem stands out as eternally hopeful:

> We shall o'ersweep the grave to meet...

According to Emma Petrie and others, that is exactly what Lady Arabella and Sir William did. In death, they overcame all opposition to their love, "o'ersweeping" the grave to meet in the lovely, haunted gardens of Lambeth Palace.

# The Wrotham House Wraith

Throughout his lifetime, Viscount Charles Lindley Wood Halifax (1839–1934) held a great interest in authenticated ghost stories. His collection of strange tales was published after his death as *Lord Halifax's Ghost Book* (1936). One of the stories in that compilation is particularly interesting because it was first told by one woman and then corroborated by another, quite independently. The event itself took place in the spring of 1880 in a historic house at Wrotham, a few miles from Maidstone in the county of Kent.

A well-to-do family by the name of Brooke was invited by friends to spend a week at the ancient house. The husband, a captain and adjutant of the Royal Engineers at Chatham, was unable to leave his duties, but he encouraged his wife to take their five-year-old daughter. The little girl had been ill, and Captain Brooke thought that a change of scenery would benefit her. Mrs. Brooke agreed, and decided that their nurse would accompany them as well.

Mrs. Brooke, her daughter and the nurse arrived at Wrotham House on a Saturday, with plans to stay until the following Saturday. They were given rooms in a distant wing of the house, at the extreme end of a long passageway. The bedroom and dressing room were not connected, so Mrs. Brooke decided that the nurse would sleep in the dressing room, while she and her daughter shared the bedroom.

That evening, Mrs. Brooke stayed up very late visiting with her hostess. As they finally began making their way to bed, a single chime of the clock indicated that it was 1 AM.

"My goodness! Already Sunday morning!" Mrs. Brooke remarked to her friend as she turned to walk down the long hall that led to her bedroom. She was no doubt looking forward to a good night's rest, but later recalled that it was not to be so:

> The instant I reached my room I was struck by the vault-like coldness of it and anxiously approached my child to see if she felt it. She appeared to be perfectly warm and was sleeping soundly, but for more than an hour after I had lain down beside her I shivered and shook with cold.

The next morning, when the nurse came into Mrs. Brooke's bedroom, it was evident that she too had suffered a bad night. Her face was pale, her eyes were rimmed with red and she wore a haunted expression. When Mrs. Brooke questioned her, the nurse said that she had been kept awake until one o'clock by someone playing pranks. Whoever it was had repeatedly opened her door, laughed evilly, then gone away and returned. Mrs. Brooke noted that the nurse could have put an end to the nonsense by simply locking her door.

"I did, twice," the nurse said, "but soon afterwards it was opened again."

Mrs. Brooke told her that she had been dreaming. She might have even convinced her of it. But after breakfasting with the other servants, the nurse returned to her employer even more agitated than she had been before.

"Oh, ma'am," she said to Mrs. Brooke, "is it not too bad? These rooms are haunted and the doors can never be kept shut before one o'clock!"

Again, Mrs. Brooke attempted to calm her. In the end, she promised that she would make some inquiries about whether there was any foundation to the servants' superstitious stories.

Mrs. Brooke was as good as her word. When she returned from church that morning with her hostess, she asked the woman about the house. She asked which was the oldest wing of Wrotham, and whether it had any haunted rooms. At that, the hostess and her daughter exchanged a knowing glance and became visibly uncomfortable.

"Yes, there is a haunted room," the woman finally admitted, "but we will not tell you which it is, as you might imagine things."

Mrs. Brooke replied that she believed she already knew which part of the house the phantom frequented.

"My nurse was frightened by the ghost last night," she said.

The hostess offered no more information, but did say that she would allow her under-housemaid to keep the nurse company that night, if it would make her feel more secure. Mrs. Brooke accepted the offer, and the arrangements were made.

That evening, as they prepared to retire, Mrs. Brooke told her nurse and the other servant girl to leave the door to their room open.

"Try to go to sleep without thinking of any foolishness," she advised them. "You know, of course, that ghosts do not exist."

Though she spoke bravely, Mrs. Brooke securely locked her own door that night and took the extra precaution of putting a chair back underneath the handle. She fed the fire until it was roaring and tried her best to stay awake. But at some point she fell asleep. She awoke to hear the clock striking 12 and found that she was unable to go back to sleep as the room was growing colder by the minute. She lay shivering in the dark for several minutes. Then she became aware of footsteps in the hallway. Mrs. Brooke was horrified when she realized that they had stopped directly outside her bedroom door.

> Then I heard a slight fumbling, as it were, with the handle of the door, which was thrown open quite noiselessly. A pale light, distinct from the firelight, streamed in, and then the figure of a man, clothed in a gray suit trimmed with silver and wearing a cocked hat, walked in and stood by the side of the bed farthest from me, with his face turned away from the window. I lay in mortal terror watching him, but he turned, still with his back to me, went out of the door uttering a horrid little laugh and walked some paces down the passage, returning again and again.

Despite the terror that she felt in the night, by morning Mrs. Brooke had nearly convinced herself that she had merely suffered a nightmare. Still, that evening she asked the nurse to sleep on the sofa in the bedroom that she and her daughter were sharing. She did not tell the young woman about her frightening experience of the previous night.

At midnight that night, the clock struck loudly and Mrs. Brooke awoke. Softly, she whispered the nurse's name to determine whether she was awake. The nurse answered that she was. Both women lay awake in the darkness in the room that was growing increasingly colder. Then there was a sound in the passage outside the door and the nurse spoke.

"I hear steps, ma'am. Do you?"

"Yes," replied Mrs. Brooke. Then, bravely, she added, "I will get up and meet it, whatever it is."

But, try as she might, she could not rise. Mrs. Brooke felt as if she was "bound to the bed." She felt what little courage she had leave her as the door swung noiselessly open and the terrifying specter in gray entered the room. The ghost acted exactly as he had the night before, letting loose a diabolical laugh before he left. The difference was that this time the nurse witnessed it as well. She saw the wraith, she heard the footsteps and the evil laughter and she too felt incapable of movement or speech while it was all happening.

This time, Mrs. Brooke would not be able to convince herself, the nurse or anyone else that the ghost was merely a product of the imagination.

The next morning, Mrs. Brooke announced to her hostess that she would be leaving. It was only Tuesday—she had planned to stay until Saturday—but she was certain that her nerves could not withstand another night in Wrotham House. At this announcement, the hostess suddenly became much more forthcoming about the resident ghost.

"You've nothing to fear," she assured Mrs. Brooke. "He only appears three times, only to strangers, and he's never done a bit of harm."

But Mrs. Brooke could not be convinced. She left that morning with her daughter and the nurse, and swore that she would never spend another night in the cursed house.

A year or two later, by the time she related the story to a French bishop, Mrs. Brooke had learned that the family living at Wrotham House had suffered from ghostly visitations for some 75 years. The apparition, according to tradition, was the spirit of a man who had murdered his brother in that bedroom and then thrown his body out of the window.

Mrs. Brooke told the bishop all of this and her full version of the story. Then she added that the nurse who had been with her would no doubt corroborate what she had just reported. And so it was arranged for the nurse to send a written account of her recollection. Regarding the events that took place on their last night in Wrotham House, the nurse wrote:

> I never like to think of it, but this is what I remember. You asked me to sleep in the room with you and Miss M., and at twelve o'clock we both woke and heard the hour strike and both said how cold it was, and then we heard the steps in the passage and you said, "I will get up to see what it is," but you did not, and then the door which you had shut and locked was opened and a man dressed in gray came in and stood looking out the window and there was a bright light and I was so cold and my nightdress was quite wet; and then he

went away and came back twice again and there was a wicked laugh at the door and the steps going away and I think you said, "Thank God it's all over," and we both cried, and you lit the candle and there was the door wide open and you said, "We will pack up and go home tomorrow, I can't stop here without the Captain." I think that was all.

It was more than enough to authenticate the story of the Wrotham House wraith, making it worthy of inclusion in Lord Halifax's prized collection of strange tales.

# The Monk's Eternal Walk

All of England seems to abound with the somber phantoms of nuns and monks. The country's stormy religious history is likely to blame for this multitude of restless religious spirits—in particular, Henry VIII's dissolution of the monasteries and convents following his 16th-century break with the Roman Catholic Church. The buildings were frequently converted into private homes, but it was common for them to be haunted by the silent, robed ghosts of those who had dared to take a stand against their oppressors. The story of one such house was originally published in the late 19th century, in an anonymously penned collection called *Ghostly Visitors*. It was retold in Pauline Saltzman's book, *Ghosts and Other Strangers* (Lancer Books, 1970).

It all began when a British couple identified only as "Mr. and Mrs. V—" decided that they wanted to leave the bustle of London behind and find a peaceful place in the country. They began to search for a suitable house by placing advertisements and applying to house agents. It wasn't long before their excitement turned to disappointment. There were few places on the market, many were outrageously expensive and the rare properties that were appropriately appointed and priced were snapped up before they even had the opportunity to consider them. Eventually a friend told them of a place in Worcestershire that seemed to be a custom fit. It was a tastefully furnished house, "beautiful and commodious." The shooting was said to be excellent and the surrounding countryside absolutely picturesque. As for the rent being asked—it was far less than expected.

Mr. and Mrs. V— drove out to the country to investigate the house. It was everything that had been described to them and more. The low rent raised some suspicions—surely there was *something* the matter with the place—but a thorough inspection revealed no problems whatsoever. All in all, it appeared to be the perfect house. The couple readily agreed to the rental terms and declared themselves the happy new tenants of the grand old country house.

Once they had settled in, Mr. and Mrs. V— adopted the habit of spending their evenings in the richly appointed sitting room that was part of the entrance hall. There, they could relax amidst the luxurious antique furnishings, and marvel at the suits of armor and ancestral portraits that served to complete the decor. At the far end of the room, a staircase rose to meet a gallery. At either end of the gallery were doors that led to bedrooms.

Mrs. V— was particularly fond of what she referred to as the "antiquated-looking place," and spent as much time as possible in the room. She was there alone one evening, working on a piece of petit-point, when she heard the bedroom door at one end of the gallery first open and then slam shut with a violent crash. She looked up and saw a man walking slowly along the gallery. He was dressed in the brown habit of a Carmelite friar. Mrs. V— was too shocked to move as she watched the monk move along the gallery, but when he opened the door at the opposite end and disappeared through it, she was able to act.

"There are burglars in the house!" she screamed.

Mr. V—, who had been enjoying an after-dinner cigar on the veranda steps, came rushing into the room.

"He's up there!" said Mrs. V—, pointing at the far bedroom door. "I just saw him go through!"

Without waiting to hear another word, Mr. V— charged up the stairs and through the door. After a few minutes, he returned. He reported that he had searched the bedroom thoroughly and had found no intruder.

"Well," said Mrs. V—, "there must be a secret passageway, then—some way of escaping the room. I *know* what I saw. The man was plainly visible!"

Mrs. V— spent the next several evenings staked out in the sitting room, strategically positioned so that she had a good view of anyone who might dare to sneak along the gallery. She did not see the intruder again until many nights later, when a friend was visiting.

Mr. and Mrs. V— and their friend, a colonel in the Royal Artillery, had retired to the sitting room following dinner. They were in the midst of a pleasant conversation about the house when they were interrupted by the sound of a slamming door from above. All three turned to face the gallery, and saw the brown-robed friar making his way slowly toward the opposite door.

"Do you see?" shrieked Mrs. V—. "Do you see?"

Both Mr. V— and the visiting friend saw the figure.

"This fellow may be one of a band of counterfeiters, who has adopted this disguise for the purpose of frightening you away from the place," said the colonel. "Such things have happened before, you know. Come along, V—, let's have a thorough examination of the place."

Mr. V— and the colonel conducted an exhaustive search of the house, but they turned up no sign of counterfeiters or any other type of trespassers. The mystery remained unsolved.

One week later the monk made his next appearance. The V—s were entertaining again—this time, two young military men who had found the story of the visiting monk highly entertaining.

"I hope we get a look at him," one said. The subject had all but been forgotten by 10 PM, when the door at the far end of the gallery unexpectedly crashed open.

There he was again: the mysterious monk. He moved along the gallery so slowly this time that Mrs. V— was able to see the mournful expression on his lined face. For the first time, she wondered if the figure might actually be a ghost, rather than a living person. When she expressed this opinion, her young guests teased her mercilessly.

"Come off it, Mrs. V—," they laughed. "This is the 19th century! More likely your monk is the lover of one of the housemaids."

To prove that the intruder was of this world, the young visitors decided that a trap should be set. Before the next evening arrived, they tied a length of rope to the balustrade on one side of the gallery and nailed it to the wall on the opposite side. They then settled in to enjoy an evening's conversation and merriment, knowing that if the monk appeared, he would be snared by the trap.

When, by 10 PM, the monk still had not appeared, someone commented that "the ghost [won't] favor us tonight, just because we are prepared for him." But as the clock struck 11, the wag was proven wrong.

There was no noise this time, no slamming of the door. But Mrs. V— spotted the monk all the same, and drew everyone's attention with her dramatic gasp. She pointed to the gallery, and everyone turned to look. They all saw the solemn figure in the brown Carmelite robe slowly moving toward the door opposite the one from which he had emerged. All who watched him held their breath, waiting for the moment when the mystery man would become entangled in the trap they had set. They were astonished when it did not happen, when the monk passed through the bedroom door with perfect ease.

"Perhaps the nails have fallen out of the wall," some-one suggested. Everyone raced up the stairs to see if this was the case. What they found in the gallery was that their rope was as securely fastened and as tautly strung as it had been when they left it. Yet the monk had walked through it as though it did not exist. At the end of the evening, the men were all the more mystified than they had been before, and all were more willing to entertain Mrs. V—'s ghostly theories.

As for Mrs. V— herself, if she wasn't convinced that night that the friar was a ghost, she certainly was by the following afternoon...

Determined to get to the bottom of the mystery, Mrs. V— invited one of the neighbors over for tea. She was a woman who had lived in the area for many years, someone well-versed in the history of the place. Mrs. V— asked her, very directly, if she knew of any unsavory stories associated with their house.

"Why yes," the neighbor replied. "I have heard it said that [your home] was once a monastery. When that rapacious tyrant, King Henry VIII, drove away the monks and nuns from their various abodes, no one was spared. All were equal. By royal mandate, the monks were banished from the monastery that is now your home. All obeyed, except one, and he positively refused to leave the house to which he was so deeply attached."

"And was he permitted to remain?" Mrs. V— asked.

"No. He was murdered," said the neighbor.

The mystery of the monk had been solved.

Soon afterward, Mr. and Mrs. V— decided that country living, especially with a ghost, was not for them. They vacated the house, which was once again advertised in need of tenants. "In need of house mates," might have been a more appropriate phrase, since the grand home seemed to already have one permanent tenant: the sorrowful monk, crossing the gallery in his eternal walk.

# 5
# Victorian Mysteries

*≈*

*The puzzling...*
*The bizarre...*
*The unexplained...*
*The Victorians loved a*
*good mystery, and the*
*stranger the details, the*
*more delightfully intrigued*
*they were. From tales of*
*time travel to claims of*
*wildly exotic inventions,*
*people of the 19th century*
*were always willing to*
*consider the impossible...*

*≈*

# Puzzling Discoveries

The 19th century brought with it an abundance of significant discoveries in all areas of science and technology, but many were of the less traditional kind, too—findings so strange and mystifying that they could not be easily categorized or explained by the scientific community. They were discoveries of the seemingly impossible, the illogical, the absurd. Because they flew in the face of a widely accepted foundation of cautious theory and knowledge, they tended to be dismissed by most people. But not by all. Those who loved mysteries and those who believed that phenomena of all kinds deserved to be documented, whether or not they made sense, managed to preserve some fascinating accounts of the Victorian era's most puzzling discoveries.

Charles Fort (1874–1932)—who would become known as "the father of modern phenomenalism"—collected and catalogued thousands of accounts of such oddities, all the while railing against the scientific community that refused to acknowledge his work. He referred to his discoveries as "strange, damned, excommunicated things...excluded...buried unnamed and undated in science's potter's field." His belief was that phenomena should be considered genuine, whether or not they could be proved or explained, and he devoted most of his life to collecting information that might have been overlooked by traditional scientists.

Fort's *Book of the Damned* listed over 1000 of these curiosities. Though it was not published until 1919, many of the incidents listed took place in the previous century. They included such interesting items as the discovery of a gold thread embedded in stone. A small story in the June 22, 1844, *London Times* reported that some workmen who had been quarrying rock near the Tweed River made the discovery. The thread had been found at a depth of eight feet in rock that obviously predated the invention of thread. Science ignored the find. Charles Fort included it in his book.

Another mining discovery that fascinated Fort happened in Kingoodie Quarry, in the north of England, around the middle of the 19th century. A block of stone cut from that quarry was found to have a nail within it. The point of the nail, which projected out of the stone, had been eaten away by rust, but a full inch of the nail as well as the nail head were perfectly preserved within the rock. Fort noted that while it was impossible to say exactly which part of the quarry the stone had come from, it could not have been from the surface—for the quarry had been worked for more than two decades at the time the mysterious nail was found.

Another "nail story" collected by Fort originated in the *Springfield (Mass.) Republican*. It told of a man named Hiram DeWitt of Springfield, who had returned home from California with a piece of auriferous quartz the size of a man's fist. On Thanksgiving Day 1851, he brought his souvenir out to show it to a friend. As the quartz was passed from hand to hand, it dropped to the floor and split in two. Inside, firmly embedded in the center of the mass, was a perfectly cut iron nail. The *Republican* noted that the nail was entirely straight, with a perfect head, and was about the size of a six-penny nail. "By whom was that nail made?" the news article asked. "At what period was it planted in the yet uncrystalized quartz?" These questions baffled scientists. Only Charles Fort offered a theory: "...ages ago, when auriferous quartz was forming—super-carpenter, a million miles or so up in the air—drops a nail..."

More than 30 years later, in 1885, coal miners in Austria found a strange metal block in a tertiary coal seam. When the object was analyzed, it was found to be composed of iron carbon, with a small quantity of nickel. It had the pitted appearance that was supposedly characteristic of meteorites and so, for a time, it was classified as a fossil meteorite. But eventually even scientists had to admit that the object was too exact a geometric form to be that. It was a cube, with two opposing convex faces, carved all the way around with a deep incision. Its presence in the ancient seam raised numerous questions. Had the material come from the earth or fallen from the sky? Had it been shaped by man, or some other intelligent force? The scientists who examined the thing could reach no conclusion, but offered instead three possible explanations that were included in *Book of the Damned:*

> 1) That it was of true meteoritic material, and had not been shaped by man; 2) That it was not of true meteoritic material, but telluric iron that had been shaped by man; 3) That it was true meteoritic material that had fallen from the sky, but had been shaped by man, after its fall.

Fort dismissed the findings, claiming that one had to ignore much of the data (specifically, the geometric form, the object's presence in an ancient deposit, material as hard as steel and man's inability to work with such material in Tertiary times) to entertain any one of the three proposed explanations.

Charles Fort found most of his information by scouring back issues of newspapers and scientific journals. They provide a good source for any researcher of oddities: a few minutes with an old roll of microfilm will almost always produce one or two "strange-but-true" tales. For example, an 1852 letter to the editor of an English newspaper detailed one reader's "geological puzzle." The man had hired a crew to break up limestone for the purpose of making lime. At one point, one of the men came to him with an object that had been found in the center of one of the stones. It was an iron or steel instrument, the thickest end of which was a socket. The letter writer claimed that the socket part was "filled with the same deposition of limestone that surrounded it," and that "there was not the smallest crack or flaw in the piece of rock." He also wrote that "the workmanship of the instrument would have done credit to any of our modern mechanies [sic], it being perfectly round, and as well finished as if it had been done in a turning lathe."

Also in 1852, the June 5 issue of *Scientific American* reported that a beautifully engraved, bell-shaped vessel had been blasted out of a wall of solid rock in Dorchester, Massachusetts. The article noted that the carving and inlaying were "exquisitely done by the art of some cunning workman," and declared that the matter was "worthy of investigation, as there is no deception in the case." Despite the declared worthiness of the case, the origin of the vase was never determined.

Thirty-nine years later, to the month, an Illinois woman cracked a lump of coal for her fire and found that the two broken pieces were linked together by ten inches of gold chain. The end pieces of the chain remained embedded in the coal, which came from a mine in the south of the state. Considering that such an object was of workmanship beyond the means and skill of the primitive people who may have lived in Illinois when coal was forming there, the discovery of the chain was a great mystery.

Of course, not all mysterious discoveries were of objects out of their customary place. Sometimes the stories were of human remains being found in seemingly impossible locations. In 1855, a California miner searching for gold in Table Mountain found a complete human skeleton instead. The discovery was made at a depth of approximately 200 feet, and from between 180 to 200 feet from the mouth of the tunnel that was being cut. Years later, in Kansas, a human skull embedded in solid rock was found in the western portion of the state. In characteristics, it most closely resembled Neanderthal man. An article in the *St. Louis Republican* pointed out, however, that "Neanderthal bones were found in loam only two or three feet beneath the surface. This skull was discovered in solid rock."

While the Victorians unearthed their fair share of such mysteries, they also left behind the occasional quandary for citizens of the 20th century to solve. In July 1945, there was a case that, according to the newspapers, "had the best medical and police brains of Great Britain stymied..."

In the rubble of a bombed site behind a Methodist chapel in Liverpool, a seven-foot-long metal cylinder had been unearthed. It was a curious thing, riveted solidly shut. Eventually someone grew suspicious enough to call the police. Bolts were pried off, the cylinder was opened and a macabre discovery was made. Inside, there lay the fully clothed corpse of a man. The dead man's clothing and personal items suggested that he had been entombed in the cylinder since the late 19th century.

According to Harold T. Wilkins' book, *Strange Mysteries of Time and Space* (Ace Star Books, 1958), the police who investigated the matter recorded the following information for the coroner's inquest:

> A postcard was found on the body, bearing the name of T.C. Williams, and written by a man named A.E. Harris on July 3, 1885. The postmark was blurred and cannot be deciphered. There was a handkerchief, not marked with initials or laundry signs. Also a worn signet ring, hall-marked 'London 1859.' No money was in the corpse's pockets, and no other valuables. A brooch was also found in the cylinder.

The coroner stated that, since the man had been dead for as many as 60 years, it was impossible to determine the cause of death. However, he did decree that the man had "worn clothing of good mid-Victorian quality" and that he had no doubt "that the man had crawled into the cylinder." The coroner's report made no mention that the dead man could not have then bolted the cylinder shut behind him, thereby sealing himself in his metallic tomb.

According to Wilkins' book, the Liverpool police made little effort to determine whether a murder had taken place, and spent even less energy attempting to identify the dead man. Was the corpse the "A.E. Harris" who wrote the postcard? We will likely never know. The famous skeleton in a cylinder remains an unsolved mystery—another puzzling discovery linked to the strange Victorian era.

# "Jonah" Bartley

"ANOTHER JONAH" screamed the headline of the 1891 newspaper. Below it, in bold, smaller type, "The Plain Story of James Bartley's Sojourn in the Belly of a Whale." It was a story of truly biblical proportions, told by the crew of a whaling vessel that had just arrived in New Bedford, Massachusetts, after two and a half adventurous years in the South Atlantic. They had with them a crewman named James Bartley, who claimed to have survived 36 hours in the stomach of a large whale. Though it sounded too fantastic to believe, the captain and each member of the crew vouched for the veracity of Bartley's statement. The people of New Bedford, the world's leading whaling port, were enthralled by the story and hungry for every detail that Bartley and his shipmates were willing to provide.

Their whaling vessel was named the *Star of the East*. Bartley was no stranger to the boat or to the work of a whaler; the 38-year-old man had twice left the port of New Bedford on the same ship. He must have enjoyed his work—for Bartley told his curious friends and neighbors that he was eager to set out on another whaling voyage and was simply waiting for another such opportunity to present itself. His enthusiasm seemed incredible, given the adventure he had just endured.

In February 1891, the *Star of the East* was searching for whales in the vicinity of the Falkland Islands. One morning, the lookout sighted a whale approximately three miles away on the starboard quarter. Two boats were manned and set off in the direction of the prey. Within a short time, one of the boats was near enough to note that the whale was an exceedingly large one. The harpooner sent a spear into the great animal's side. It bellowed and then sped away, dragging the small boat behind it. The crew estimated that the whale towed them for some five miles, traveling at a great rate of speed, then turned and hauled the boat back to almost the exact location where the battle had begun.

The second boat was still there waiting. At the first glimpse of the whale's huge back rising above the surface, another spear was fired. It sank into the flesh of the whale, which began to thrash about, crazed with pain and fury. For several wild minutes, it appeared that both of the boats would be swamped and the crews drowned, but eventually the whale grew calmer. It swam away once more, this time dragging two boats in its wake.

After what the men estimated to be three miles, the whale sounded loudly and then sank beneath the surface. The lines attached to the harpoons became slack. The harpooners began to slowly draw them in and coil them in the tubs. If they were thinking that the whale had finally died, they were wrong; for as soon as the lines grew taut, the mighty animal rose to the surface and began to beat the water with its huge tail. The men tried to move the boats beyond the reach of the whale. Only one crew succeeded. The other boat was struck by the whale's nose and upset, spilling men into the frigid, black water. By the time the other boat was able to circle back and attempt to rescue the crewmen, one had already drowned and James Bartley had vanished altogether.

When the injured whale had finally exhausted itself and lay dying, the men searched the surrounding waters as thoroughly as they could for Bartley. His body could not be found, and it was assumed that he had been struck by the whale's tail and sent into the murky depths. Saddened and spent, the survivors rowed back to the ship.

The whale, after the considerable battle, had died. Within several hours its massive body was lying by the ship's side. The men used axes and spades to cut through the flesh to secure the fat. The enormous job could not be completed in a day. It wasn't until the next afternoon that they had worked their way down to the animal's stomach, which was to be hoisted onto the deck. As workmen labored to fasten a chain around the huge pouch, they were startled to notice discernable movement within. There was some creature trapped inside the whale's stomach, something still showing spasmodic signs of life. The pouch was hauled up to the deck and carefully sliced open to free whatever sea creature it was that was clinging to life within.

It was James Bartley.

The sailor was doubled up and mercifully unconscious, but alive. The crewmen laid him out on the deck and doused him with seawater. This action revived his body, but not his mind. As Bartley regained consciousness, he began to rave like a madman. The captain of the ship ordered that Bartley be placed in the captain's quarters until he was well. For two weeks, he stayed there, muttering and wailing incoherently, all the while being treated very carefully by the captain and officers of the ship. Eventually he regained possession of his senses. By the end of the third week, James Bartley had recovered entirely from his shock and resumed his regular duties. When enough time had passed, he shared the details of his terrifying experience with his fellow shipmates.

Bartley recalled the sensation of being lifted into the air by the nose of the whale and then splashing down into water. The next thing that he remembered was a deafening rushing sound, which was followed by sudden darkness. He felt himself slipping along a smooth passage of some sort that seemed to move and carry him forward. An instant later he was in an area that afforded him slightly more room, surrounded by a yielding, slimy sac that shrank away from his touch. It was then that Bartley understood that he had been swallowed by the whale, and it was then that he began to lose his mind. According to the newspaper report,

> He could breathe easily, but the heat was terrible. It was not of a scorching, stifling nature, but it seemed to open the pores of his skin and to DRAW OUT HIS VITALITY. He became very weak and grew sick at his stomach. He knew that there was no hope of escape from his strange prison. Death stared him in the face, and he tried to look at it bravely, but the awful quiet, the fearful darkness, the horrible knowledge of his environment and the terrible heat finally overcame him, and he must have fainted, for the next he remembered being in the Captain's cabin.

Later, Bartley always said that he probably would have lived inside his horrible house until he starved to death—

after all, he lost his senses through fright and not through a lack of air. That he experienced such mind-altering fright proved to all the crew what a terrifying ordeal he had been through, since Bartley was well known for his steely nature. Still, it was many weeks before the courageous sailor could pass a night without suffering nightmares about angry whales and the sensation of being imprisoned.

Though James Bartley eventually overcame the psychological wounds inflicted by his ordeal, he bore a physical scar that would always remind him, and everyone he met, of what he had endured. According to the newspaper report, Bartley's skin, having been exposed to the gastric juices in the whale's stomach for so many hours, underwent a striking change. His face and hands were bleached to a deathly whiteness and the skin was heavily wrinkled, "giving the man the appearance of having been parboiled." It was said that the sailor never recovered his natural appearance, but was little bothered by it.

"He is in splendid spirits and apparently fully enjoys all the blessings of life that come his way..."

What other attitude could a man have after surviving such an unimaginable ordeal?

# The Shades of Jack the Ripper

*It is the autumn of 1888. On a damp, moonless night, a middle-aged prostitute wanders through the filthy, narrow streets of one of London's notorious East End slums. Her goal is to earn enough to buy a pint or two at a local pub and a bed in one of the vermin-infested lodging houses. There's a thick fog swirling around her feet, seeping through her shabby clothes, and it would be lovely to be indoors...*

*Suddenly, as if out of nowhere, a man appears. He is uncommonly well-dressed for the neighborhood; his dapper cloak and hat are silhouetted against the yellow gaslight. But, gentleman or not, he seems to be looking for someone just like her. She smiles a little, revealing a number of gaps where teeth ought to be, and thinks that she might also buy herself a nice mince pie...*

It began on August 31 with the brutal slaying of Mary Nichols. It ended when Mary Jane Kelly's butchered body was discovered on November 9. For exactly 10 weeks in 1888, the neighborhood of Whitechapel in London's East End was terrorized by the most famous serial killer of all time. "Jack the Ripper," as he was dubbed, murdered and eviscerated at least five prostitutes in a poverty-stricken hive that swarmed with unfortunate humanity and yet, somehow, he managed to avoid detection.

More than a century later, the killer's identity is still not known. "Ripperologists" continue to study the facts of this sinister Victorian murder mystery; they pore over the coroner's reports, the witnesses' testimonies, the case file from Scotland Yard. But most tend to overlook other records—accounts that are less official, less tangible, but there all the same. They are the shades of the terrible thing that happened—the atmospheric impressions of the violence and trauma that was inflicted upon five hopeless women and the fear that gripped thousands of others. The Whitechapel murders spawned an extensive collection of supernatural tales, dating back to the time of the murders. While such stories may never help to solve the coldest of cases, they are worthy of attention, all the same.

*...There was a time when it seemed that almost every person living in the East End of London knew a Ripper of a ghost story...*

This was something Peter Underwood discovered as he researched his book *Jack the Ripper—One Hundred Years of Mystery* (Blandford Press, 1987). Though he seldom raised the subject himself, people he interviewed about the Ripper murders frequently referred to things of a ghostly nature. It was a surprise to Underwood, who wrote:

> The average East Ender is not particularly superstitious or gullible and usually answers any story of ghostly happenings with a sharp rejoinder that leaves no question as to his or her views on such stories, but with the Ripper sites it was, and still is to some extent, quite a different matter. Here, time and time again, I was informed—without asking or raising the question of ghosts or supernatural happenings

or any special atmosphere—that of course the sites were haunted.

People seemed to accept that when such terrible things happened, they were bound to leave an impression of sorts upon the surroundings. Perhaps this acceptance made them more open to perceiving unusual events. The five murder sites were heavily associated with phenomena that included isolated screams, the eerie sound of heavy breathing and echoing, disembodied footsteps running into the distance. There were apparitions associated with the murders as well—perhaps the most famous being seen at the murder site of Catherine Eddowes, the Ripper's fourth victim.

Eddowes' body was discovered in the early morning hours of September 30, in the darkest corner of Mitre Square. It was a place that would come to be called "Ripper's Corner," and come to be known as haunted. As the decades passed, dozens of people reported seeing the apparition of Eddowes' body lying in the exact place where she was found. Her prone form appeared so real to people that they usually approached her to see if she needed help or medical attention. In every instance, when the witness was no more than a few feet from the body, it vanished before his eyes. Some people were observant enough to be able to later describe the clothing the woman was wearing and the exact position in which she lay. The description always matched that of Catherine Eddowes. Interestingly, in every case, Eddowes' specter was seen in late September. Often it was on the very anniversary of her death.

Annie Chapman, Jack the Ripper's second victim, was killed beside the steps leading down to the backyard at number 29, Hanbury Street. Following her murder, people often quickened their pace when walking down the street past the address. It may have been the unpleasantness associated with the location, or it may have been the eerie sounds that caused them to hasten along. For years, people reported hearing muffled voices and the sounds of struggle—an auditory replay of Chapman's death. Peter Underwood was told a fascinating story by a man named Thomas, who had heard the disturbing ruckus when he was a young man. Thomas, being unaware of the ghost stories, thought that he was hearing a real attack. He listened for a moment to the sounds of struggle, panting and muffled voices. Finally he decided to investigate.

> Walking very quietly, since he was wary of what he might encounter, he made his way until he stood on one of the steps that led down into the backyard where the body of Annie Chapman had been found, on the lefthand side of the steps.

> He peered round the door towards the spot where the body had been discovered. It was completely deserted but he could still hear the sounds apparently emanating from the spot he was looking at! He told me he had never felt so frightened in his life. He looked over the fence, and there was nothing there either, but in any case the further he moved from the site the less distinct were the sounds.

It wasn't until after his unnerving experience that Thomas learned that similar sounds had been occasionally heard by other passers-by.

Another man, whose name also happened to be Chapman, although he was unrelated to the victim, lived for several years at the address opposite number 29, Hanbury Street. He was witness to a different phenomenon that he eventually came to associate with Annie Chapman's murder. It began early one morning, when he looked out his bedroom window just in time to see a man and woman disappear through the doorway leading to the yard at number 29. He thought little of it, but did remember their attire: the woman was wearing a long skirt and the man had on a heavy coat and a tall hat with a wide brim. Their fashions were badly outdated, but that hardly made the couple suspect. Chapman thought no more of it.

That is, until the next time he saw them.

On the second occasion, Chapman met the strange couple on the street, early one rainy morning. He remembered them because they were dressed exactly as they had been the first time, and they were again walking toward number 29. As the man and woman disappeared through the doorway, something suddenly struck Chapman as odd. He realized that as they had passed him, they had made no sound of any kind—there had been no footsteps, no rustle of clothing, no splashing as their feet sloshed through the puddles. Chapman's interest was piqued, and he began to keep an eye out for the mysterious couple. He was curious by then; he wanted to see them again—and he would, on two more occasions.

The third time Chapman spied the man and woman, it was again from his bedroom window. Excited, he called his wife over. Mrs. Chapman hurried to the window, but arrived too late to see the couple. Her husband told her that she had been only a split second too late; he said that they had just disappeared through the door to the yard. Mrs. Chapman commented that it was odd she hadn't at least seen the door close behind them, and it was then that Chapman realized that the door had never *opened*. The spectral figures had seemed to "melt into the door and disappear."

On the fourth and final time that Chapman saw the ghosts, he was again on the street, this time with his brother. As the two men walked along, Chapman spied the phantom couple moving silently down the street approaching number 29. As they were about to pass, Chapman began to nudge his brother furiously, trying to draw his attention to the apparitions. After the couple had vanished through the door, he spoke.

"There, you saw them," Chapman said. "Who on earth are they?"

His brother replied that he had seen no one, but had heard disembodied footsteps passing by. He had assumed *that* was what Chapman had been trying to draw his attention to. Chapman had seen the couple and heard nothing, while his brother had heard them pass, but seen nothing.

In *Ghosts of London* (Jarrold and Sons, 1982), author J.A. Brooks wrote that Annie Chapman's ghost may actually have been haunting a different location—

a nearby Whitechapel pub. At least that was the claim of the landlord.

> [He was] quite certain that it was the ghost of [Annie] Chapman which haunted his pub. Anyway, he managed to get a good mention in the *Hackney Gazette* in August 1975, when he claimed the ghost for his pub, complaining of the strange gusts of cold wind that came from nowhere, and the radio that would switch itself on and off, and other more or less unaccountable happenings that took place there.

This particular report may have been somewhat more promotional than paranormal, however, given that the establishment in question was the "Jack the Ripper Pub."

Mary Nichols was the Ripper's first victim. Her dead body, still warm to the touch, was discovered before dawn on August 31. The woman's eyes were open and staring, her throat had been slashed from ear to ear and her intestines had been cut out and thrown over her left shoulder. The grisly sight must have left an indelible impression upon the two workmen who found her, as it seemed to leave an indelible impression upon the location itself. For years following the murder, people often reported seeing the rumpled form of a woman in tattered Victorian clothing, lying exactly as Mary had, with her head near a door and her feet in the road. A pale, eerie light was said to radiate from the corpse. Even at times when the macabre vision did not appear, animals were said to fearfully avoid the haunted place where the woman had long before been found.

It seems that the spirit of Mary Kelly, the fifth of Jack's victims, remained earthbound with a strong desire to communicate psychically with the living. It is not difficult to imagine that she wanted someone to understand who she was, what she had endured and, perhaps most of all, who her killer had been. Over the decades, several people have reported feeling an "affinity" for Kelly over the other doomed prostitutes. Many have claimed that the dead woman attempted to communicate with them in some way.

One man, a retired banker with a vast knowledge of the Ripper case, experienced sudden, strong feelings that Mary Kelly was with him on three different occasions. Though he was quick to admit that the episodes might have been self-induced, he was stunned each time by the power of the sensation and the inherent certainty that it was caused by Mary Kelly's presence.

In another case, an actress who was playing the part of Mary Kelly in a stage play began to experience visions of the dead woman. She felt that she had psychic contact with her, and even wondered if she might be the reincarnation of Kelly. The actress devoted a great deal of time and energy to researching the Ripper case and visiting the locations where the murders took place. Whatever message Mary Kelly was trying to impart never came through clearly, however, and eventually the psychic incidents ceased.

John Morrison, who self-published a book entitled *Jimmy Kelly's Year of Ripper Murders*, claimed that the identity of the killer was given to him by Mary Kelly's ghost. Immediately after visiting the woman's gravesite, Morrison felt compelled to buy a large selection of old paperbacks at a rummage sale. He took them home and tried to put the books away in a small shelf—but one would not stay put. As he tried to push it into place with his foot, the book fell to the floor, open to a page that contained a fictional passage about an escaped lunatic having committed the Whitechapel crimes. Working with this idea, Morrison eventually concluded that James Kelly, a murderer who had escaped from the Broadmoor Lunatic Asylum, was the man Mary Kelly wanted exposed as Jack the Ripper.

There are some who believe that Mary Kelly's ghost was communicating with people within hours of her death. The testimony of Mrs. Caroline Maxwell, a witness at the Coroner's Inquest into Kelly's murder, would tend to support this. Mrs. Maxwell said that she saw Mary twice between 8 and 9 AM on the morning of November 9. The first time, she had stepped out the front door to watch for her husband on his way home from work. She saw Mary across the street then, and spoke to her. Mary said that she was not feeling well, and that she had just vomited. Mrs. Maxwell went back inside then, having told Mary that she "could pity her feelings."

Mrs. Maxwell went shopping then, to get things for her husband's breakfast. When she returned, she saw Mary Kelly again. This time, Mary was standing outside of the Britannia public house, talking to a man. He wore dark clothes, the witness said, although she was not able to offer much more of a description of him. "We are accustomed to see men of all sorts with women," she said. Mrs. Maxwell was not even willing to "pledge [herself] to the kind of hat" the man wore.

Before Mrs. Maxwell began her testimony, the coroner had advised her sternly, "You must be very careful about your evidence, because it is different to other people's." Indeed it was, for the period of time in which Caroline Maxwell claimed to twice see Mary Kelly was actually several hours after the woman had been murdered. Mrs. Maxwell never once wavered in her testimony, though, and seemed very credible and sure of her facts. Could it have been, in those early hours, that Mary Kelly's spirit was already trying to shed light on the case? Could it be that she managed to conjure the image of her killer, along with her own, in front of the Britannia? It is a pity that Caroline Maxwell never paid much attention to the man—for he may have been the monster Jack.

Elliot O'Donnell, the author of several books on British ghosts and hauntings, once noted that spectral images seen in the location of a violent death rarely last for more than 50 years after the event itself. It is as though they are charged with emotional energy that drains away over time, eventually causing the apparition to fizzle away into nothing. Then, of course, there are cases where the landscape itself changes, due to redevelopment, and can no longer provide a suitable stage for the ghostly re-enactment. Given these assumptions, and the amount of time that has passed, the ghosts of Jack the Ripper's victims may soon go, or be gone already. One hopes that the spirits of these tragic women can now rest easily, knowing that they will never be forgotten. The very knowledge of what happened to them so long ago is enough to haunt people forever.

# Strange Victorian News

Victorians were known to love a fantastic story—and the stranger the details, the more likely they were to believe that the tale might actually be true. In an era when scientific discoveries were revolutionizing industry, transportation, communications, health, religion and every other aspect of daily life, people grew increasingly credulous. Accepting such wild theories as evolution and witnessing such amazing things as x-ray technology required that a person kept an open mind. It was a time when anything seemed possible—particularly when one learned about it in that reliable daily source of information: the newspaper.

The smallest, most random sampling of 19th-century newspapers always manages to produce a few weird tales. It would seem that in those days, the oddest of accounts from the most questionable of sources was considered newsworthy. From the papers of the day, from a time before supermarket tabloids, come these few examples of the strange Victorian news...

First, a small item from the *London Examiner*, October 29, 1842:

> EXTRAORDINARY FISH IN THE THAMES
> The lovers of the marvelous have been gratified by the finding of an enormous eel in the river Thames and the capture of a small whale, a very unusual visitor here, during the last few days. On Saturday

the ballastmen engaged in one of the Trinity lighters brought up in a scoop what they first took to be a large snake, but was soon ascertained to be an eel, measuring nine feet six inches in length, and two feet in circumference. The captain of a Waterman steamer offered a large sum for the eel, but it was finally disposed of to a fishmonger in Shadwell. The ballastmen stated that the eel snorted and barked at them like a dog when they first took it out of the water.

For people who were more interested in sideshow spectacles than in barking eels, an interesting case was reported in Florida in 1883. The story ran in an October edition of the *Jacksonville Times*.

### HALF HUMAN, HALF ALLIGATOR

Perhaps the greatest living curiosities now in existence in this country will pass through this city on their way to Cincinnati and Louisville next Tuesday. About two years ago Charles Lewis, in passing through the state, discovered about 15 miles below St. Augustine, a family of white persons, consisting of John McDonald, his wife and five children. Two of the children he found to be half human and half alligator. He at once contracted with the parents to give him the management of the children, and agreed to pay them $25 per month to take care of them until such time as he saw fit to take them away. A few weeks ago Mr. Lewis returned to the state for the purpose of taking the children north, and on

Wednesday arrived in this city to arrange for their transportation...

These children are now 9 years of age, and have never been to exceed 10 miles of their home, and consequently have never been placed on exhibition. Their bodies, arms and heads from the hips up are perfectly formed, while from the hips down they present the identical appearance of an alligator, having a perfectly formed tail about five feet in length, together with the hind feet and legs of the gator. They crawl around on their hands and feet, converse intelligently, and seem to enjoy life very much. They live part of the time in water, which they enjoy very much, using their tails while swimming the same as the alligator, to propel their bodies. They are healthy, good-looking children, and outside of their love for the water their general mode of living is the same as that of other human beings.

Apparently, being born as a half alligator was no hardship. Sadly, the same could not be said for the California girl who, in 1886, made headlines as

### A HUMAN BATTERY

Modesto, California, Sept. 8—Fifteen miles from this town resides a young lady who has developed into a perfect electric battery. A few evenings ago, while she was about to retire, she extinguished the light in her room, and with a quick motion rolled back the bed covering, when, lo and behold! the bed immediately was turned into a sheet of fire. The young lady, much frightened, screamed "Fire!" and at the same time grabbed the bed covering in her arms.

When the other members of the family arrived at the door of the room, they found her standing in the middle of the room in what seemed to be a flame of fire; but no sooner had the bed clothes been taken from her arms than the flames disappeared. Experiments made by the young lady since have proved that she has become possessed of a vast amount of electricity, which shows itself at every opportunity. The young lady is not at all satisfied with the phenomena, as it requires the greatest caution on her part to keep from starting up a small bonfire by the slightest movement of her hands.

As science and religion continued to do battle for the minds and souls of the masses, it was ancient superstition that often prevailed. Countless newspaper stories demonstrated that age-old fears of evil and darkness and things unknown remained alive and well...

In *Strange Magazine* (#5, 1990), writers Mark Chorvinsky and Mark Opsasnick contributed an article entitled "A Field Guide to the Monsters and Mystery Animals of Maryland." Several of the entries came from the Victorian era, including the following.

In the November 29, 1883, Frederic, Maryland *News*, a man with the initials "R.B." wrote a letter to the editor describing a mysterious entity that he had witnessed flying through the air one early morning. "[It was] a monstrous dragon with glaring eye-balls, and mouth wide open displaying a tongue, which hung like a flame of fire from its jaws..." Two years later, not far away, an article was written about a man who was frightened by "a large white fiery eyed monster" near what was reputed to be a haunted silver mine. Also from Maryland—a state seemingly cursed by an abundance of monsters—came the story of the "Goblin Damned." The story of these mysterious creatures ran in the March 17, 1876, *Montgomery Sentinel,* revealing shocking eyewitness evidence: it seemed that "questionable shapes" had been seen on the railroad bridge crossing Big Seneca Creek in Montgomery County.

Of course, there remained a large segment of the Victorian population who opted for the more traditional versions of frightening creatures—and it's impossible to find a more time-honored representative of evil than the devil himself...

### EXTRAORDINARY OCCURRENCE

*London Examiner,* January 17, 1855—Considerable sensation has been caused in the towns of Topsham, Lympstone, Exmouth, Teignmouth and Dawlish, in the south of Devon, in consequence of the discovery of a vast number of foot-tracks of a most strange and mysterious description. The superstitious go so far as to believe that they are the marks of Satan himself; and that great excitement has been produced among all classes may be judged of from the fact that the subject has been descanted on from the pulpit.

It appears that, on Thursday night last, there was a very heavy snowfall in the neighborhood of Exeter and south of Devon. On the following morning the inhabitants of the above towns were surprised at discovering the footmarks of some strange and mysterious animal, endowed with the power of ubiquity, as the footprints were to be seen in all kinds of unaccountable places—on the tops of houses and narrow walls, in gardens and courtyards, enclosed by high walls and railings, as well as in open fields.

There was hardly a garden in Lympstone where these footprints were not observable. The track appeared more like that of a biped than a quadruped, and the steps were generally eight inches in advance of each other. The impression of the foot closely resembled that of a donkey's shoe, and measured from an inch and a half to (in some instances) two and a half inches across. Here and there it appeared as if cloven, but in the generality of the steps the shoe was continuous, and from the snow in the center remaining entire, merely showing the outer crest of the foot, it must have been convex.

The creature seems to have approached the doors of several houses, and then to have retreated, but no one has been able to discover the standing or resting point of this mysterious visitor...Many superstitious people in the above towns are actually afraid to go outside their doors after night.

For those who wished for something a little more thrilling than some footprints (satanic though they may have been) in the snow, there came a fabulous story in September 1890, featuring—quite literally—a cotton-picking witch.

### TENNESSEE SUPERSTITION
A Whole Community Stirred Up by a Yarn About Witchcraft.

The greatest excitement ever known is being created in Weakley County, Tennessee, by the appearance of a witch in the family of Frank Hass, living three miles southeast of Greenfield in the Ninth district. Mr. Hayes's [sic] granddaughter, about 14 years of age, being the object upon which the wicked phantom has centered.

The young lady is prostrated and hundreds are flocking there to see the effects of the attack, which, strange to say, no one can explain. She is perfectly sane until she hears them coming, when she goes into violent spasms, and declares she can hear roaring as like distant thunder, and she can see animals making their way to her.

Now comes the strangest part of the story, and a number of the most reliable men in the county can vouch for this as a fact, there being eye-witnesses to the same. After each attack a small roll or bat of cotton is found clinging to the victims' neck just above her breast, and the most incredible ones have held their hands very lightly against her neck and found, after the spell is over, beneath their hands the mysterious cotton. When the rumor first went out that this strange case was in the country the people all ridiculed such, but the excitement is now at its height on account of all being at a loss to account for the whole affair.

The family stated to your correspondent that they have been threatened by so-called witches in the past. Notwithstanding how purely absurd this may seem to anyone who has not seen the entire affair, it is certainly a mystery, to say the least.

Finally, there is a terrifically entertaining story from the September 12, 1880, *New York Times,* which demonstrates the Victorian ability to embrace the wonder of science while maintaining great suspicion regarding the motives of scientists themselves:

### AN AERIAL MYSTERY

One day last week a marvelous apparition was seen near Coney Island. At the height of at least a thousand feet in the air a strange object was in the act of flying toward the New Jersey coast. It was apparently a man with bat's wings and improved frog's legs. The face of the man could be distinctly seen, and it wore a cruel and determined expression. The movements made by the object closely resembled those of a frog in the act of swimming with his hind legs and flying with his front legs. Of course, no respectable frog has ever been known to conduct himself in precisely that way; but were a frog to wear bat's wings, and to attempt to swim and fly at the same time, he would correctly imitate the conduct of the Coney Island monster. When we add that this monster waved his wings in answer to the whistle of a locomotive, and was of a deep black color, the alarming nature of the apparition can be imagined. The object was seen by many reputable persons, and they all agree that it was a man engaged in flying toward New Jersey.

About a month ago an object of precisely the same nature was seen in the air over St. Louis by a number of citizens who happened to be sober and are believed to be trustworthy. A little later it was seen by various Kentucky persons as it flew across the state. In no instance has it been know to alight, and no one has seen it at a lower elevation than a thousand feet above the surface of the earth. It is without doubt the most extraordinary and wonderful object that has ever been seen, and there should be no time lost in ascertaining its precise nature, habits and probable mission.

That this aerial apparition is a man fitted with practicable wings there is no reason to doubt. Someone has solved the problem of aerial navigation by inventing wings with which a man can sustain himself in the air and direct his flight to any desired point. Who is this adventurous flyer and what is his object? are questions of immediate and enormous importance. Of course, the first impulse of the unreflecting mind will be to exclaim that the mysterious flyer is an aeronaut who has invented practicable wings, and is secretly experimenting with them before making his invention public. This is directly at variance with the known habits and customs of aeronauts...

Why has not the inventor patented his invention and had himself duly written up by the press? The reason is obvious. The flying man is engaged in some undertaking which he cannot safely proclaim. In other words, he is an aerial criminal, a fact which explains the cruelty and determination visible on his countenance, and what can be the nefarious object which this probable wretch has in view? It cannot be simply theft and robbery, for it would manifestly be impossible for him, in his flying costume, to perpetuate burglary or highway robbery, or to pick pockets. It cannot be plumbing, for obvious reasons, neither can it be the sale of books published by subscription only. Yet the flying villain must have an object, and we have a right to assume that only a peculiarly nefarious object could induce a man to fly to New Jersey or St. Louis in hot weather and without an umbrella or mosquito net...

Oddly enough, as with all of these newsworthy Victorian tales, the mystery of the flying frogman remains unsolved...

# Dellschau, Keely and Spear: Inventive Minds

The 19th century brought with it a seemingly endless parade of lifestyle-changing inventions. Such developments as photography, electricity, telephones and automobiles promised a future where any dream could be made a reality through the miracle of science. Of course, some merely dreamed of fantastic creations, while others attempted to bring them to life. Charles Dellschau, John Keely and John Murray Spear were three Victorian gentlemen belonging to the latter category. They devoted their lives to pushing the boundaries of what was possible—and however strange and questionable their theories were deemed to be, each of these men managed to leave an indelible, original mark on the Victorian era.

In the year 1890, no one in the city of Houston, Texas, would have taken Charles August Albert Dellschau for a creative genius. He was 60 years old at the time, a nondescript widower working as a clerk in the saddle-making shop of his stepdaughter's husband. Dellschau was unremarkable enough until that year, when he left town on a mysterious vacation that lasted several months. When he returned to Houston, those who knew him said that he had changed. The man who had once been merely withdrawn had become reclusive, avoiding human contact whenever possible. Dellschau seemed nervous and fearful. He spoke to few people and trusted none. By the turn of the century, Charles

Dellschau had retired, affording himself the opportunity to become even more isolated. For the final 23 years of his life, Dellschau stayed in self-imposed exile in his attic room, shunning even the extended family with whom he lived. Claiming that he feared for his life, the hunched old man spent nearly every moment in his attic. He slept there, he ate there and it was there that he worked in secret on the project that consumed him for more than three decades. It was a series of intricately detailed illustrations and notebooks that he had begun upon returning to Houston in 1890—a body of work that would continue to inspire wonder and debate decades after his death. At the time of his death, Dellschau had filled 12 large notebooks with more than 5000 drawings, cryptic notes and fascinating mixed-media collages, all pertaining to the theme of aviation.

The focus of each of Dellschau's drawings was a fantastical, mechanized flying machine, referred to in the notes as "aero." There were illustrations of more than 100 aeros throughout the 12 notebooks, each one shown from a variety of angles to display an amazing range of functions and working parts. They were whimsical-looking, brightly decorated things, and Dellschau enhanced their circus-like appeal by bordering his artwork with colorful, geometric motifs, flamboyant banners and columns of stripes or checks. The ornamental details were elaborate, yet it was obvious that even greater attention had been paid to illustrating the mechanical and functional technicalities. The aero designs appeared to be incredibly complex, featuring such advanced concepts as air compression, shock absorption and gas conversion.

Charles Dellschau's heirs took little interest in the collection. The books were left in the attic and it was there that they remained until the late 1960s, when the house was cleared of debris following a fire. The dozen volumes documenting Dellschau's obsessive interest in aeronautics were then piled beside the curb with the garbage and might have been lost forever had an enterprising trash collector not taken an interest. He salvaged the books and sold them to a local antiques dealer for the sum of $100. From the dealer's shop, four of Dellschau's books were purchased by an art collector named Dominique de Menil. In 1969, de Menil lent the unusual books to the University of St. Thomas for an exhibition on the history of flight. Charles Dellschau's remarkable body of work was beginning to gain some attention, but the secret story behind it was yet to be revealed.

The word that was often used to describe Dellschau's folk art was "cryptic." The man's painstakingly detailed illustrations of elaborate flying machines, clippings of newspaper articles (he called them "press blooms"), ciphers, acronyms and endless writings combining Dellschau's broken English and native German created the effect of being scrambled pieces of some great, mystifying puzzle. In some notes, Dellschau acknowledged that he was working in a code that might someday be broken. "You will—Wonder Weaver—you will unriddle these writings. They are my stock of open knowledge," he wrote in one of his books.

As it happened, the "Wonder Weaver" who would decipher Dellschau's notes and reveal his secrets was a Houston artist by the name of Pete Navarro. Navarro first encountered the eccentric artwork when it was exhibited at the University of St. Thomas. When he discovered that Dellschau had produced other books, aside from the four on display, he tracked them down and purchased them for himself. With eight of the volumes in his possession, Navarro began an intensive course of study that eventually led to what has been described as the most detailed analysis of Dellschau's work ever produced. Part of the process involved translating German phrases, researching names and places indicated in the drawings and analyzing the symbolism found within the books. In the end, Navarro believed that he had decoded Dellschau's carefully encrypted message—and uncovered an amazing piece of early aeronautical history.

According to Dellschau's veiled writings, he had once been a member of a secret society known as the "Sonora Aero Club." The organization of 62 members had formed in California in 1850, brought together by their common interest in aeronautics. The group was composed mostly of German and English men, all of whom were intensely secretive about the club and its activities. This clandestine behavior may have been the members' choice, but it was more likely imposed upon them by the society that funded them—a mysterious organization referred to only as "NYMZA." Either way, the rules were strict, the activities were highly classified and members employed "brotherhood" names to keep them from being identified to the outside world. Although the reason for the secrecy was unknown, the Sonora Aero Club's mission was very clear: they intended to design, build and fly navigable aircraft.

Charles Dellschau's records claim that they were successful.

In Dellschau's notes, he wrote that of the 100-plus crafts that he drew, at least eight—with such fanciful names as "Aero Goosey," "Cripel Wagon" and "Aero Buster"—were actually constructed and test-flown by the club. Flight was made possible by a remarkable gas known as "NB" or "Supe," small amounts of which were able to both lift and propel the heavy craft. The formula for the creation of Supe was guarded more secretly than anything else in the clandestine organization. It was known to only one member, Peter Mennis, who was reluctant to see it used for any aero designs other than his own. In the end, Mennis' greed may have been his, and the group's, undoing. He either disappeared or died in the early 1860s, leaving the Sonora Aero Club grounded.

Some believe Mennis may have been murdered and that he was not the first club member to meet such a fate. According to Pete Navarro's research, a man named Jacob Mischer was dispatched by club members after he threatened to go public and profit from one of his own designs, the "Aero Flyerless Gander." That was how strictly the rules of the Sonora Aero Club were enforced.

Such extreme consequences for betrayal would explain why no member of the club ever spoke out, and it would explain Charles Dellschau's paranoia during the years he spent creating his secret notebooks. But it does not explain everything. How was it that the club was able to conduct countless test flights without ever being spotted by someone on the ground? The answer, according to some theorists, is that they *were* seen *and* reported—but that the witness sightings were easily dismissed. UFO enthusiasts now believe that the abundance of mysterious sightings around Oakland, California, in the late 19th century may have been owing to the activities of the Sonora Aero Club.

The club continued to design aeros for years after Peter Mennis' disappearance, but, without the power of Supe, they were unable to take to the air. Eventually, they gave up hope of ever rediscovering the formula and disbanded. Still, if what Dellschau documented is to be believed, what the Sonora Aero Club achieved—a full half-century before the Wright brothers made history at Kitty Hawke in 1903—was nothing short of amazing. Had they never left the ground, their accomplishments of design would still have been noteworthy. According to Pete Navarro, Dellschau's illustrations portrayed such contemporary ideas as "hydraulic, pneumatic and retractable landing gear, shock absorbers, inflatable pontoons for landing on water, hot gas/air jets for thrusting, powered wheels for moving on land and even parachutes and other safety devices for emergencies."

But the question remains: was Dellschau working from memory, or from a gifted imagination? We may never know. But whether he truly was a member of the Sonora Aero Club or simply an eccentric man imprisoned by his own irrational mind, Charles Dellschau was genuinely talented, and one of the great visionaries of his time.

John Keely was another Victorian who was unquestionably talented, but to this day it remains to be proven whether his talents lay in the field of cutting-edge science or in the realm of fraud. Either way, Keely met a receptive audience when he announced in 1871 that he had tapped into a limitless new source of energy.

The timing could not have been more perfect. The late 19th century was a time when energy was sorely needed to meet the unrelenting demands of growing industry. Society needed an inexpensive new form of power to operate its ever-increasing number of mills and factories—and John Keely was offering just that.

He called it an "etheric generator" and described it as "a device which disintegrates the etheric force that controls the atomic constitution of matter." No one understood what that meant, but everyone wanted to believe what Keely said it could do. He claimed that, with his generator, one quart of water would be all the fuel needed to send a train from the east coast to the west coast—and back again. Two quarts of water would propel a steamship from New York to Liverpool. "A bucket of water," promised Keely, "has enough of this vapor to produce a power sufficient to move the world out of its course."

People were sold. It didn't matter that Keely had no scientific background to speak of because everyone *wanted* to believe in his promise of cheap, limitless power. The wealthy were even willing to put money behind that belief, and in no time John Keely had raised one million dollars in capital. The former carpenter, violinist, fur trapper and magician finally answered his one true calling when he formed the Keely Motor Company in 1872.

At first, things looked promising. Within two years, Keely had produced a working model of his etheric generator and had demonstrated its abilities before an audience in Philadelphia. It was only a demonstration, however;

Keely offered no detailed explanation of how his invention worked, nor did he indicate that practical applications of his new energy source were in the offing. The Philadelphia show was the first of many such events; it was a flashy method of distraction used by Keely to placate investors when they grew impatient waiting for profits. As the years passed, the shows grew more spectacular. By the power of the mysterious machine, thick ropes were torn apart, great weights were lifted, bullets were fired through 12-inch planks and iron bars were twisted or broken in two.

Eventually, carnival-like showmanship was not enough to satisfy Keely's increasingly disgruntled stockholders. In the late 1880s, they dragged him into court, where a judge ordered that the plans for the etheric generator be revealed. Keely ignored the court order, choosing to spend time in jail rather than divulge his secrets.

John Keely *never* gave away his secrets. Even when demonstrating an invention, his explanation of its workings would be rife with pseudo-scientific babble that often sounded impressive but usually meant nothing. Still, he convinced many—including respected, mainstream scientists—that he had discovered something great. But he was never able to perfect his sensitive machine to the point where it could be marketed, or even successfully operated by anyone other than Keely himself. Finally, he ran out of time. In 1898, John Keely died of pneumonia, taking his secrets with him to the grave. The Keely Motor Company had existed for 26 years and never manufactured a single product.

Throughout John Keely's career, *Scientific American* magazine had been skeptical of his claims and critical of his methods. In the March 25, 1884, edition, it was written, "It is difficult, indeed, to consider seriously this alleged invention, or justly characterize the inventor, who, in this age, not only assumes to get something out of nothing, but would hide all his methods and processes and affect more than the mystery of the alchemists of the early ages." Furthermore, staff from the magazine who had witnessed some of Keely's demonstrations were convinced that everything he did could easily have been achieved by employing a hidden source of compressed air. Not surprisingly, the *Scientific American* staff were among those who invaded Keely's laboratory immediately following his death. The etheric generator was already gone, taken by a supporter of Keely's who hoped to continue his work. But it didn't matter. The secret wasn't in the machine; it was in the building itself.

The investigators discovered false ceilings and floors that hid a system of switches, belts and linkages to conventional motors that were secreted away in the basement. Also in the basement was a three-ton metal sphere, believed to have been used as a reservoir for compressed air. That was all it took for the people from *Scientific American* and others to decide that Keely had been an all-out fraud.

But was he?

According to Frank Edwards' book *Stranger Than Science* (Ace Star Books, 1959), the pipes connected to the sphere "were inadequate to have operated at the pressures indicated by the performance of the machine." Moreover,

Keely had never really hidden the sphere; he had showed it to several people over the course of the years, including one reporter who later wrote an amazing article about having witnessed Keely levitate the huge sphere using his "Aerial Navigation System," which consisted of a mechanized belt with a wire attachment. So there were those who still believed.

And there are those who still do, to this day.

It would seem that an inventor who left behind no inventions should soon be forgotten, but John Keely remains well known today. Some insist that he was ahead of his time, employing theories in his experiments that were not truly understood until late in the 20th century. Others, of course, insist he is famous only for having committed one of the greatest stock frauds of all time. More than 100 years after his death, Keely continues to inspire both supporters and detractors—and the debate regarding the authenticity of his work rages on.

John Murray Spear was another Victorian who claimed that he would bring a society-altering new machine into the world. Like Keely, Spear dealt with many nonbelievers. But, quite unlike Keely, no one questioned his integrity. Spear was always considered to be utterly honest and ethical, if not entirely sane.

Spear was born in 1804. By his mid-20s, he had been ordained as a Universalist minister and had his own congregation in Barnstable, Massachusetts. As the years passed, he served other congregations and other causes as well. He campaigned vigorously for the rights of prisoners and women, and called for an end to the death penalty. Throughout his life, Spear was also an active and outspoken abolitionist who spent years as an operator on the Boston portion of the Underground Railroad. Ultimately, Spear gained less attention for this lifetime of good work than he did for a single bizarre announcement that he made in 1853. That was when John Murray Spear told the world that a "Congress of Spirits" had chosen him to mechanically construct the New Messiah.

Spear had left the Universalist Church by that time and had joined the spiritualist movement that was sweeping the nation. He believed himself to be gifted as a trance medium and claimed to be the channel for many notable spirits, including Emmanuel Swedenborg, Benjamin Franklin and Thomas Jefferson. According to Robert Damon Schneck's article "The God Machine," in the May 2002 *Fortean Times*, these distinguished departed had organized themselves into a committee of sorts:

> Spear began producing automatic writing which proclaimed him to be the earthly representative for the "Band of Electricizers." This was a fraternity of philanthropic spirits directed by Benjamin Franklin and dedicated to elevating the human race through advanced technology. Other groups that made up the "Association of Beneficence" were the "Healthfulizers," "Educationalizers," "Agriculturalizers," "Elementizers" and "Governmentizers," each of which would choose their own spokesmen to receive plans for promoting "Man-culture and integral reform with a view to the ultimate establishment of a divine social state on earth." The Electricizers began speaking through Spear, transmitting "revealments" that ranged from a

warning against curling the hair on the back of the head (bad for memory) to plans for electrical ships, thinking machines and vast circular cities.

There was one task that took priority over all others, however: the realization of what the Electricizers called "heaven's last, best gift to man." It was the construction of the New Messiah—a mechanical and spiritual creation that has since been referred to as John Murray Spear's "God Machine."

Spear's invention was meant to bring about a new revelation of scientific and spiritual truths through a mechanical being that would "correspond to the human organism." The philosophy behind it was that all "merely scientific" developments of motive power were superficial and useless, as they required artificial sources of energy to operate. Conversely, the "New Motor" would be able to absorb atmospheric electricity, thereby acting as independently as did the human body.

Spear and a handful of supporters chose a location high atop a hill in Massachusetts and went to work. Spear would enter what he called a "superior state," or trance, where the spirits could communicate detailed instructions to him. Since there was never a plan or blueprint in place, the group was directed one step at a time. Eventually, over the course of nine months, at a cost of $2000, an odd-looking machine took shape. It covered the surface of a large dining room table and consisted of an impressive collection of metallic shafts, arms, spheres and plates. There was a large flywheel, several magnets within the machine and steel balls suspended from its various metal appendages. Beneath the table, two metallic legs connected the New Messiah to the earth.

Spear's miraculous machine was complete. Now, according to the Electricizers, it needed only to be born.

Spear went into a deep trance, during which time a woman known only as "The Mary of the New Dispensation," who had been chosen to be the New Messiah's mother, began to exhibit signs of pregnancy. On June 29, 1854, Mary spent two hours in labor on the floor in front of the machine. When her pains ended, she rose and touched the contraption. Members of the group claimed that, at that moment, the New Messiah became animate. Spear announced to the world the arrival of "the New Motive Power, the Physical Savior, Heaven's Last Gift to Man, New Creation, Great Spiritual Revelation of the Age, Philosopher's Stone, Art of all Arts, Science of all Sciences, the New Messiah."

The editor of a Boston spiritual periodical called the *New Era,* a friend of Spear's, was similarly effusive. He wrote:

> [A]fter about nine months of almost incessant labor, oftentimes under the greatest difficulties, we are prepared to announce to the world, first that spirits have revealed a wholly new motive power to take the place of all other motive powers. And second, that this revelation has been embodied in a model machine by human cooperation with the powers above.

Impartial witnesses were somewhat less impressed than were Spear and his associates, noting that the machine was quite inanimate in their presence. Spear pointed out that it was only a baby, and needed time to develop and be nurtured by the New Mary. At some point, even Spear and his followers grew impatient waiting for their progeny to reach its full potential. It was collectively decided that a change of air and scenery might speed the maturation process along. The machine was dismantled and moved to Randolph, New York—but it was never again seen. John Murray Spear claimed that an angry mob broke into the building where the New Messiah lay in storage, destroyed all the pieces and scattered them so that they could never be repaired and reassembled. There are no historical records of such an event, leading others to speculate that the disappointed and humiliated Spear simply disposed of his invention in the quietest of fashions.

Andrew Jackson Davis (page 64) had, at one point, written a lengthy critique of the project. In it, he had defended Spear's character while gently suggesting that his New Machine had been born of something other than spirit directives. Seemingly searching for something kind to say, Jackson noted that however useless the New Messiah was, it was indeed marvelous in appearance. In noticing this, Jackson may have struck upon something quite relevant. The machine was not a god—but was it art?

In his *Fortean Times* article, Robert Damon Schneck arrived at a similar conclusion. Though John Murray Spear did not reach the goal he set out to accomplish, he did achieve something significant; in Schneck's words, Spear created "a statue that expressed the human urge for transcendence." Unfortunately, it was a statue that did not survive for future generations to behold.

# Without a Trace

Throughout time, storytellers have spoken of people who have vanished without leaving any explanation or trace of evidence. The Victorian era was no exception—in fact, as with stories of any type of strange phenomena, it may boast even more than its share. In *Strange Disappearances* (Lancer Books, 1970), author Brad Steiger cited several 19th-century incidents of vanishing, including the fascinating and unexplainable tales of James Burne Worson and Charles Ashmore.

James Burne Worson was an amateur English runner who made a fatal wager with his friends in September 1873. Worson bet them that he could jog to a neighboring Warwickshire town and back, a distance of more than 40 miles. The friends set out to settle the bet, riding in a wagon while Worson ran behind them. The three who were riding were jeering Worson in a good-natured way when suddenly, right in front of their eyes, "the man seemed to stumble, pitched headlong forward, uttered a terrible cry and vanished." The runner disappeared before he hit the ground and was never seen again.

Charles Ashmore's case was different in that there was no one present to witness his disappearance, but he left behind some incredible evidence. Ashmore was the 16-year-old son of an Illinois farm family, and he went missing on November 9, 1878. On the evening of that day, he had been sent to the spring to fill a drinking bucket with fresh water. When he failed to return, his father and older sister took a lantern and went out in search of him.

According to the story, a light snow had been falling, which made it easy to follow Ashmore's tracks. The father and daughter walked along the path until they reached a point where, impossibly, the footprints came to an end. They did not appear to double back or proceed. They came to a full stop halfway between the house and the spring, as though at that particular spot, Charles Ashton had ceased to exist.

The family was grief stricken and, for several months afterward, was tortured by the vague sound of their lost son and brother calling to them from the vicinity of where he was lost. Several times, family members would try to follow the voice, but it was faint and directionless and they had no success.

Those are only two cases, but according to Michael Harrison, the author of *Vanishings* (New English Library, 1981), the Victorians were even more prone to disappearances than were people of other eras. He wrote:

> Of all such periods, the decade between 1880 and 1890, both in Europe and America, endured what must be the most concentrated and prolonged attention from What [sic] ever it is which conducts the removal of human beings from this world.

This particular time period included a strange case that Harrison refers to as "the epidemic of the Vanishing Londoners." Beginning in 1881, in the London suburbs of East Ham and West Ham, an alarming number of people were reported missing. The similarities and differences in the cases were fascinating. There was no pattern in terms of age or gender. Young and old alike disappeared, males as easily as females. What linked many of the cases were witnesses reporting that they had seen the person in question talking to a strange old woman just before they went missing. Occasionally, the missing people mentioned having premonitions that "something" was going to happen to them. But it was never determined exactly what that "something" turned out to be.

In his book, Harrison also wrote of other times in Victorian history when people disappeared in large groups or series—including August 1869, when 13 children disappeared from Cork, Ireland, and the summer of 1892, when there were "so many strange vanishings in Montreal, Quebec, that the newspaper headline 'Another Man is Missing' became commonplace."

No one has ever been able to explain where these lost souls have gone—but it has been said that, in at least one rare case, one of the missing came back. From an article by Scott Corales in *Unexplained Mysteries, Special Report #2* (GCR Publishing Group, 1996):

> In 1950, a New York City paper allegedly carried a four-line news item relating the death of a pedestrian hit by a car near Times Square. The car had apparently been unable to stop and a crowd of

onlookers ran to offer assistance to the unfortunate victim, one Rudolf Fenz, who was pronounced dead.

An uneventful story? Only on the surface. According to many, it was the details that were not reported in the paper that made Fenz's death a fascinating case. The man was wearing Victorian clothing—a Prince Albert coat, narrow trousers and buckle shoes—that had not been fashionable since the previous century. He had appeared as if out of nowhere and seemed frightened and confused. People had watched as Fenz gaped at the skyscrapers that surrounded him and shrank in terror from the automobiles that honked and sped past. It was only a few moments before the panicked man took a wrong step into the path of an oncoming vehicle.

When the police attempted to identify Fenz, the mystery grew. In his pockets, they discovered several crisp but long-outdated bank notes, calling cards printed with his name, an invoice from a livery stable and a letter postmarked 1876. But the address on the calling cards had been converted to shops some decades before, and the livery stable had been out of business for a generation. Finally, the authorities found a telephone listing for a Rudolf Fenz, Junior—but when they called it they found that he had been dead for many years. His widow made an interesting comment to investigator Hubert V. Rihn of the missing persons division. She said that her husband's father had gone missing as a young man. It had happened in 1876, she said. Fenz, Sr., had been out for a walk to the local tobacconist...

Rihn compared the woman's story with 74-year-old missing persons report. He discovered that a Rudolf Fenz had gone missing in 1876, while on a trip to buy some tobacco. He had been wearing a Prince Albert coat, narrow trousers and buckle shoes. The case had gone unsolved and Fenz had never been seen or heard of again.

That is, until 1950, when he took a wrong step in front of a speeding car...

# Victorian Maritime Mysteries

Since the earliest days of ocean travel, there have been legends of ghostly ships and mysterious events taking place at sea. One such story belonging to the Victorians was that of the *Marlborough*, a vessel that set sail from Littleton, New Zealand, in January 1890, carrying a cargo of wool and frozen mutton and a crew of 23 men under the command of Captain J. Hird. Two weeks later, she was sighted on course in the Straits of Magellan. Then she vanished. An official search was made for the ship in the spring of 1890, but it was unsuccessful. As fate would have it, it was a full 23 years before the *Marlborough* was seen again—and her discovery would then only serve to intensify the mystery of her disappearance.

In 1913, the British ship *Johnson* sighted a seemingly abandoned vessel drifting aimlessly in the waters off the coast of Chile. The unidentified ship's sails were in tatters; her masts were green with mold. As the setting sun blazed red across the western horizon, the *Johnson* cautiously approached the mystery ship. Every detail of what followed was recorded by the *Johnson*'s captain, and the story was later printed in the November 13, 1913, edition of a New Zealand newspaper:

> We signaled and hove to. No answer came. We searched "the stranger" with our glasses. Not a soul could we see; not a movement of any sort. Masts and yards were picked out in green—the green of decay. The vessel lay as if in a cradle. It recalled the "Frozen

Pirate," a novel that I had read years ago. I conjured up the vessel of the novel, with her rakish masts and the outline of her six small cannon traced with snow. At last we came up. There was no sign of life on board. After an interval our first mate, with a number of the crew, boarded her. The sight that met their gaze was thrilling. Below the wheel lay the skeleton of a man. Treading warily on the rotten decks, which cracked and broke in places as they walked, they encountered three skeletons in the hatchway. In the mess-room were the remains of ten bodies, and six others were found, one alone, possibly the captain, on the bridge. There was an uncanny stillness around, and a dank smell of mould, which made the flesh creep. A few remnants of books were discovered in the captain's cabin and a rusty cutlass. Nothing more weird in the history of the sea can ever have been seen. The first mate examined the still faint letters on the bow and after much trouble read, "*Marlborough, Glasgow.*"

Something had killed every member of the *Marlborough*'s crew—and had done so so swiftly that the men remained at their posts or at their leisure, leaving no sign of a disturbance. The ship, with its skeleton crew and cargo, had then been left adrift in the South Pacific for more than two decades.

When the *Johnson* arrived at her destination, the captain made a full report of his crew's eerie discovery. An investigation followed, but no conclusion regarding the lost ship's fate was ever reached.

Nearly a decade earlier, in the frigid waters of the North Atlantic, far from where the *Marlborough* would meet her strange fate, a ship by the name of *Ellen Austin* made an eerie discovery. She had set sail in England and was halfway to her destination of St. John's, Newfoundland, when her crew sighted an unidentified schooner. The schooner wasn't moving and failed to answer the hails of the *Ellen Austin*. When the two ships finally met, Captain Baker of the *Ellen Austin* took four members of his crew and boarded the mystery vessel with weapons drawn.

According to author Dale Gilbert Jarvis' article, "Mystery Ships of the North Atlantic," in the March 2002 issue of *FATE* magazine, the men were mystified by what they discovered aboard the schooner. Both the ship and her equipment appeared to be well maintained and in good condition. There were no signs of violence or struggle. But the schooner's nameplates had been removed and her log was missing and there was not a single person to be found aboard. Captain Baker was mystified, and decided that the only course of action was to take the abandoned ship to St. John's with them. He selected a small crew of his own men to sail the schooner the remainder of the way across the Atlantic. They were instructed to follow closely behind the *Ellen Austin*.

For two days, all went well. But when a violent storm crossed the path of the tandem ships, bringing with it high winds and crashing waves, contact between the two vessels was lost. Eventually, the bad weather passed and the waters grew calm. The crew of the *Ellen Austin* was once again able to spot the unknown schooner in the distance. She appeared to be drifting aimlessly, which concerned the captain. He ordered his crew to approach the other ship so that they might investigate. When finally they boarded the nameless vessel, the *Ellen Austin*'s crew was horrified by what they found.

The ship was once again deserted. The new logbook had vanished. The bunks appeared to never have been slept in.

Despite having no idea what fate had befallen his men, Captain Baker ordered another replacement crew to board the schooner. The men were reluctant, but dutifully followed orders. In his article, Jarvis described the events that followed:

> Shortly thereafter, yet another squall sprang up. The derelict schooner was traveling behind the *Ellen Austin* at a distance of ten ship lengths, but contact between the ships was again lost in the mist. When the storm lifted, the strange ship was nowhere to be seen. The *Ellen Austin* continued on its voyage, and neither the unknown vessel nor the second crew made it to St. John's. They were never seen again.

While the tale of the mystery schooner discovered by the *Ellen Austin* had some distinct elements and a particularly eerie appeal, the situation of discovering a derelict ship was far from unusual in those seafaring days. In April 1849, the Dutch schooner *Hermania* was found in good condition, with her captain, the captain's family and the crew all missing. The *Marathon* was discovered in a similar situation in 1855. The *Resolven* was discovered abandoned in 1884, leaving a mystery and a supposed curse on all vessels that attempted to fulfill her cargo delivery. The *Rescue* floated aimlessly—or, perhaps, not—through the icy seas surrounding Baffin Island in the 1860s. The crew of a ship called the *George Henry* believed that the *Rescue* stalked them, seeking revenge for having abandoned her during a severe storm. But whether cursed or vengeful or simply left behind, the list of derelicts was long. Often these lost ships were mistaken for phantom vessels in the ocean mist. This much was proven by the sharp decline in ghost ship sightings in the 1930s, after the US Coast Guard launched a campaign to locate and sink abandoned ships in the interest of water safety. Still, the folk tales of the old derelicts remained—and there was perhaps none more famous than the legend of the *Mary Celeste*.

The *Mary Celeste* was first launched in 1861, under the name *Amazon*. Within a few years, however, she had changed both ownership and name—something the superstitious sailing community considered to be bad luck. Indeed, in late November 1872, luck ran out for the *Mary Celeste*.

On November 7, the ship left New York, bound for Europe with a cargo of alcohol casks in her hold. She carried with her a crew of seven men under the command of Captain Benjamin Briggs. Briggs' wife and young daughter sailed with him as well, bringing the total number of people on board to 10. It should have been a routine passage, but, for some reason, it was not. Exactly four weeks later, 600 miles west of Gibraltar, a ship named the *Dei Gratia* found the *Mary Celeste* sailing out of control. They followed the ship closely for two hours, observing her erratic pattern carefully. Although there were no distress signals, the captain of the *Dei Gratia* could tell that there was trouble on the other vessel. After hailing her repeatedly and receiving no reply, some of the *Dei Gratia*'s crew set off in a small boat. When they reached the *Mary Celeste,* they boarded her and were amazed by what they found.

According to the legend, the ship was in first-class condition. Her cargo was in place, and her sails were set. There was plenty of food and water in store, including a half-eaten meal laid out in the galley. The money-box had not been tampered with, and every item appeared to be in its proper place. Only the chronometer, the navigation book and the ship's register and papers were discovered to be missing. According to some reports, a lifeboat was also gone. The last entry in the ship's log had been made some 10 days before, noting that the *Mary Celeste* had passed the island of St. Mary in the Azores. The ship had drifted 400 miles and been abandoned at sea for 10 days, yet it looked as though her crew had abandoned her only minutes before the men from the *Dei Gratia* came on board. It was a mystery that could only be explained in supernatural terms.

Or was it?

Though the legend of the *Mary Celeste* grew more incredible with every passing year, the actual facts of the case have always been somewhat less remarkable. While storytellers described everything aboard being in perfect order, the court in Gibraltar, whose task it was to determine ownership of the vessel and her cargo, revealed a different story:

The galley was in a bad state, the stove was knocked out of its place and the cooking utensils were strewn around. The whole ship was a thoroughly wet mess. The captain's bed was not fit to sleep in and had to be dried.

So what might have happened to the captain, his family and his crew? Theories abound, but most of them hinge upon the questionable "facts" invented over the years. They range from time travel, alien abduction, sea-monster attack, mutiny, piracy and conspiracy, to insurance fraud, food contamination and drunkenness. (The last theory remains popular, although the type of alcohol in the cargo was of the type more suitable as an explosive than a drink.) Based upon the actual evidence, there is one hypothesis that made sense in 1872 and continues to stand up today. It is presented on the web site "Mary Celeste—Fact not Fiction" (www.maryceleste.net):

...for some reason the captain and crew panicked and took to the ship's boat. This could have been due to a mistake in sounding the pump and thinking she was sinking, or bearing in mind the nature of the cargo, there may have been a small explosion or rumbling in the cargo...[L]et's say Briggs ordered his men to abandon ship, and snatched up his navigational instruments. In great haste they all left. It may be significant that the main halyard, a stout rope three inches in circumference, was found later broken and hanging over the side. Let us assume that they were trailing behind the ship, waiting to see if she exploded. Then, suddenly, the wind took off and snapped the rope, maybe sinking the small boat at the same time. Even if it did not, it would have been difficult to keep afloat in a small boat in bad weather.

There is hard evidence to support this theory. Testimony from the inquiry stated that there were ropes hanging over the side of the ship. Although there were no lifeboats found on board, a crew member of the *Dei Gratia* located a fixing for one at the main hatch. The records of the Servico Metrologico in the Azores note that the weather deteriorated on the morning of the *Mary Celeste*'s final log entry, bringing gale force winds and torrential rains that did not ease until December 4. There was a great deal of water between decks on the abandoned ship when she was found. It is possible that the same heavy rains that swamped the small boat also quieted the volatile cargo, saving the *Mary Celeste* from fire or explosion, but decimating her crew.

Why, then—given that there were so many more mysterious cases of derelict ships—did people choose to bestow such mythical status upon the *Mary Celeste?* The reason can almost certainly be found in the work of an author who was little known at that time—a great lover of mysteries by the name of Arthur Conan Doyle. In 1884, a young Doyle wrote a short story loosely based upon the case of the *Mary Celeste,* changing the ship's name only slightly, to *Marie Celeste.* His fictional account—written to sound as though it was a factual statement—contained many of the details that were eventually adopted into the folklore surrounding the true story. "She is perfectly watertight," he wrote. "No signs of a struggle or violence are to be detected, and there is absolutely nothing to account for the disappearance of the crew." Such imaginary specifics as a bobbin of silk that remained delicately balanced upon the top of a sewing machine were later accepted to be actual facts of the case. People's imaginations were captured, and fact and fiction were blended together to create one of the most enduring legends of the sea.

In his tale, Doyle wrote of "those numerous mysteries of the deep that will never be solved until the great day when the sea shall give up its dead." Among them are the secret stories of the *Marlborough,* the *Ellen Austin,* the *Hermania,* the *Marathon,* the *Resolven,* the *Rescue* and the infamous *Mary Celeste.* Together, they will sail into history as some of the greatest maritime mysteries of the Victorian age.

# The End

GHOST HOUSE BOOKS

# Collect the Entire Series!

## United States

- ☐ 1. Ghost Stories of Washington................. ISBN 1-55105-260-1
- ☐ 3. Ghost Stories of California .................. ISBN 1-55105-237-7
- ☐ 4. Ghost Stories of Hollywood ................. ISBN 1-55105-241-5
- ☐ 5. Ghost Stories of Illinois .................... ISBN 1-55105-239-3
- ☐ 6. Ghost Stories of Texas ..................... ISBN 1-55105-330-6
- ☐ 7. Ghost Stories of Michigan ................. ISBN 1-894877-05-5
- ☐ 8. Ghost Stories of Indiana ................... ISBN 1-894877-06-3
- ☐ 9. Ghost Stories of Minnesota ................ ISBN 1-894877-07-1
- ☐ 10. Ghost Stories of Ohio ...................... ISBN 1-894877-09-8
- ☐ 18. Ghost Stories of America ................... ISBN 1-894877-11-X
- ☐ 20. Ghost Stories of Oregon .................... ISBN 1-894877-13-6
- ☐ 21. Ghost Stories of Pennsylvania .............. ISBN 1-894877-08-X
- ☐ 23. Ghost Stories of America Vol. II ............. ISBN 1-894877-31-4
- ☐ 26. Ghost Stories of New England .............. ISBN 1-894877-12-8
- ☐ 28. Ghost Stories of the Old West .............. ISBN 1-894877-17-9
- ☐ 29. Ghost Stories of the Old South ............. ISBN 1-894877-18-7
- ☐ 32. Ghost Stories of the Civil War .............. ISBN 1-894877-16-0

## General

- ☐ 2. Ghost Stories of the Rocky Mountains ........ ISBN 1-55105-165-6
- ☐ 11. Ghost Stories of Christmas .................. ISBN 1-55105-334-9
- ☐ 12. Haunted Christmas Ghost Stories ............ ISBN 1-894877-15-2
- ☐ 13. Haunted Theaters .......................... ISBN 1-894877-04-7
- ☐ 14. Haunted Hotels ............................ ISBN 1-894877-03-9
- ☐ 15. Ghosts, Werewolves, Witches & Vampires ...... ISBN 1-55105-333-0
- ☐ 16. Campfire Ghost Stories ..................... ISBN 1-894877-02-0
- ☐ 17. Halloween Recipes and Crafts ............... ISBN 1-894877-10-1
- ☐ 24. Haunted Houses ........................... ISBN 1-894877-30-6
- ☐ 25. Haunted Highways ......................... ISBN 1-894877-29-2
- ☐ 27. Ghost Stories of the Rocky Mountains Vol. II ... ISBN 1-894877-21-7
- ☐ 30. Haunted Schools ........................... ISBN 1-894877-32-2
- ☐ 31. Ghost Stories of Pets and Animals ............ ISBN 1-894877-36-5
- ☐ 34. Haunted Halloween Stories .................. ISBN 1-894877-34-9
- ☐ 36. Ghost Stories of the Sea .................... ISBN 1-894877-23-3
- ☐ 37. Fireside Ghost Stories ...................... ISBN 1-894877-40-3
- ☐ 39. Pumpkin Carving .......................... ISBN 1-894877-26-8
- ☐ 41. Romantic Ghost Stories .................... ISBN 1-894877-28-4

**Check with your local bookseller or order direct.**
**U.S. readers call 1-800-518-3541. In Canada, call 1-800-661-9017.**
**www.lonepinepublishing.com**

# About the Author

Jo-Anne Christensen is the author of the following best-selling ghost story collections. She lives with her family in Western Canada.

～

| | |
|---|---|
| *Campfire Ghost Stories* | ISBN 1-894877-02-0 |
| *Haunted Halloween Stories* | ISBN 1-894877-34-9 |
| *Haunted Christmas Ghost Stories* | ISBN 1-894877-15-2 |
| *Ghost Stories of Christmas* | ISBN 1-55105-334-9 |
| *Ghosts, Werewolves, Witches and Vampires* | ISBN 1-55105-333-0 |
| *Haunted Hotels* | ISBN 1-894877-03-9 |
| *Ghost Stories of Texas* | ISBN 1-55105-330-6 |
| *Ghost Stories of Illinois* | ISBN 1-55105-239-3 |
| *More Ghost Stories of Saskatchewan* | ISBN 1-55105-276-8 |